many full hands applaud- ing inele- gantly

Three Poetry Sequences

by

Darren C. Demaree

PRAISE FOR *MANY FULL HANDS APPLAUDING INELEGANTLY*

There are many avenues a poet may take and I am pleased that Darren C. Demaree has skillfully led me through his good work in, *Many Full Hands Applauding Inelegantly.* The poetry in his collection is representative of clear thinking and astute observations of self and surroundings. There is no battling here; as a reader, it's a pleasure to surrender to Mr. Demaree's tides and eddy's of language. Bravo! I enjoyed this collection - and will continue to enjoy it again as a touchstone of good poetry.

-Kae Sable, Managing Editor, *Dime Show Review*

Demaree's newest installment to his oeuvre continues to cement his place as a modern poetic stylist who dare not be ignored. No other poet so seamlessly weaves pathos and purposively abstract prescience into carefully weighted stanzas as this man. In a sea of endlessly beautiful poetry, each instance procures something worth quoting.

To Be Read, and Reread, and Reread

As with his other collections, each poem forms a singularity made great by its brethren placed before and after. It reads almost novel-like in its development of theme and expression and while each is excellent individually they are deeply moving when taken together. It deserves your sit-down time in an armchair, read all at once, and then multiple times after.

Demaree puts the reader in the driver's seat of emotional intuitiveness. He grasps to understand the world in a linguisticism bent enough beyond literal to become poetic without inducing catatonia as some poets might. This, alongside his residual body of work, is another instance of Demaree raising his voice (yet somehow calmly, without abrasion) above the crowd to share something worthwhile. It is upon us, as readers, to cherish such lyricism when it comes along.

- After the Pause

Many Full Hands Applauding Inelegantly is a tour de force. Written in three, devastating parts, these extraordinary poems astound me. Demaree is a poet's poet, with a grasp of the human condition in all its glorious fragility. "I think it's good for us,/to hear only a whisper of the divine/equations. We are better at grasping/ than we will ever be at holding starlight." he says in "All The Birds Are Leaving #54."

These poems, are as necessary as the air we breathe, they fly - with sound, arrows and wings - into the heart of the reader.

- *Alexis Rhone Fancher,* Poetry Editor of *Cultural Weekly.*

'Many full hands applauding inelegantly', by Darren C. Demaree, is a book of poems written from the center, how light enters a room usually from an angle, these poems, instead begin from the middle of the room and slowly find the jagged angles where light collects, giving form to the dust, the unseen of our lives. As the opener "A VIOLENT SOUND IN ALMOST EVERY PLACE #1" puts it "I gave up smoking so that there would be one less way to find me, but I failed first to erase the constellation of good, trained ears." Darren subtly maps out the peripheral contours of human life, its ease and dis-ease, the collected bits and pieces of daily living, like a strong hand reaching deep into cold waters and pulling out the warm underbelly of a river, these works deliver themselves on a level that has much to offer, if you listen closely you can hear the chime of a resonant heart in motion, it is a life force on the move in each of these poems.

"We were not sentenced, we were gifted these trials by the perfect number on the perfect day. We are the most beautiful fraction & every effort to delay or count differently weighs the sky down, pushes it harder against our thickened chest." This is what I mean by working from the middle, the center of things, grafting meaning's deepest pull onto the skin, every poem here has something to teach, in the musical sense, how notes operate by leaning into each other, the painful but perfect fit of chord after chord, the ear learns it because the heart already knows it.

"We are sewn beauty", Darren writes, "that does not mean we cannot meet the oil and the orphan of our star's best intentions, that we exist, that our hearts are soft enough for real magic to become planted in each of our bones." It's almost as if we are listening to a phone conversation between Charles Simic and Jorie Graham, the surreal and the salvific all at once rushing through and filling the room with linguistic light.

One doesn't walk away from this book, one walks towards it. And having seen what lies inside, stitched across each page, pulsing with life and all of the jagged undersides of the unseen, the unspoken, one can't help but applaud, with the many full hands of the human heart.

- Anti-Heroin Chic

This mountainous collection of poetry was rewarding to scale. Demaree weaves personal and human experience together, exploring themes of danger and hope, adversity and relationships, loss and mental illness. We join the author on this journey of discovery, learning more about the unknown "you" that follows along with us—at times intimate, friends or family, at times the poet himself, and at other times the reader.

Refreshing bits of humor are sprinkled throughout, giving us a chance to come up for air between heavy revelations. Demaree smoothly transitions from honest reflection on mental illness with lines like, "I have no bounce on the pills. I have only fear off of them," to poking subtle fun at his own persona with lines like, "there is only so much I can do about being ornery & thirty-one at the same time."

I enjoyed this book and found myself reading straight through titles and sections, letting the poems flow one into the next and form a picture that was worth waiting for. This collection will leave you pondering your own life in the bigger scheme of things, perhaps to conclude as Demaree does, to "never rise above a mountain that could be magic, if only we allowed it to be."

-Ani Keaten, Unbroken Journal

In the newest collection by Darren C. Demaree, *Many Full Hands Applauding Inelegantly*, the narrator moves through three poetic sequences wherein the poems focus on the many forms contrast in this world, a world where we leave the chorus for the song, where we split ourselves apart from the impossible places we sometimes find ourselves in. Expansive in their compact form, these poems whisper straight-forwardly of violence, love, and a deep desire for home.

-*Erin Elizabeth Smith*, author of The Naming of Strays

I've always thought of poems as little mechanisms. Here, Demaree has created an impressive number of little love mechanisms. Love Machines. Love Engines even -- love engines in their thumping violence and inelegance, their startling power. Each perfect part, its perfect purpose. Here we have a book full of tiny perfect little love engines. Love cams creating, each love piston pumping, powering this expansive collection. I read in envy. I read in awe. I read in love.

-*Nik De Dominic*, author of Your Daily Horoscope

8th House Publishing

Montreal, Canada

Copyright © 8th House Publishing 2016
First Edition
ISBN 978-1-926716-41-1

Published worldwide by 8th House Publishing.
Front Cover Design by 8th House Publishing
Designed by 8th House Publishing.
www.8thHousePublishing.com

Set in Garamond, Franklin Gothic and Caslon.

LIBRARY AND ARCHIVES CANADA CATALOGUING IN PUBLICATION

Demaree, Darren C., author
    Many full hands applauding inelegantly / Darren C. Demaree.

Poems.
ISBN 978-1-926716-41-1 (paperback)

    I. Title.

PS3604.E56M36 2016   811'.6   C2016-907333-5

MANY FULL HANDS
APPLAUDING
INELEGANTLY

by

Darren C. Demaree

For Steven Casimer Kowalski, who taught me long ago to be as much of myself as humanly possible. Pursuing that goal taught me to be as human as possible, which ultimately led to the three Humanist sequences included in this book. I love myself and I love you (reader) much more because of my friendship with Steve.

CONTENTS

ଷ ✋ ଚ

A VIOLENT SOUND IN
ALMOST EVERY PLACE

ଷ ✋ ଚ

Darren C. Demaree

A VIOLENT SOUND IN ALMOST EVERY PLACE #1

Here I am, distant
from the sky,
surrounded by fire

& the residue of fires,
the apocrypha gibberish
of those always willing

to escape as part
of something, as a note
in any song.

I gave up smoking
so that there would be
one less way to find me,

but I failed first
to erase the constellation
of good, trained ears.

- 8 -

A VIOLENT SOUND IN ALMOST EVERY PLACE #2

Bowled over
by the swing
of thought, I

rattle eclipses
with frenetic
yearning to be

so alarmingly
different that
we write new

theories of self
& dance. I
wait for silence

to create moves
of no energy
& no regret.

A VIOLENT SOUND IN ALMOST EVERY PLACE #7

Away from the processional, I see you
un-cloud, I see you genuinely laugh
at the tide of time, the context of a laugh

in the same context of death, salmon
& penny gum, the skillet of all of those
& your laughter is the best snake oil

for those of us with mud in our mastery
of the human experience. I believe in you.
I believe in all of us. I do not know why.

A VIOLENT SOUND IN ALMOST EVERY PLACE #11

Durable float, un-easy flower
in such heavy water, the bearing
of the bowl determines

that if you touch the sides
you will float again to the middle.
If you have any petals at all,

angle them to the outskirts,
the table deserves to be pretty,
too. Pity the color of the water,

its slosh against the ceramic
world will never provide more
than context for your elegant song.

A VIOLENT SOUND IN ALMOST EVERY PLACE #12

Spasm force, uncontrollable
& yet so much stronger than
the quiver of your lips, the drool
that is never quite contained
by your flapping mind. I own
the speed of my own tongue.
I own nothing, very little else
inside the strange republic
of my soulless body. I think,
therefore, I can create a world
pressed against my own heart.
I think, therefore, I need no
voice to be whole for your burial.

A VIOLENT SOUND IN ALMOST EVERY PLACE #16

It is strength
leaving you,
affording me

a unique power
to be silent
while you

prattle on
through your
weaknesses

& the exclamation
of a reality
you took a break

from molding.
I imagine you
out of breath.

A VIOLENT SOUND IN ALMOST EVERY PLACE #17

Small laughter,
what is it like
to be perfect

among the stove
& ridicule
of outrageousness?

I choose you
to be both restraint
& full religion.

A VIOLENT SOUND IN ALMOST EVERY PLACE #18

Teacup
& summer dress,

heels, heels,
stocking feet,

sure night of this
republic,

I admire
your stray page

your un-innocence,
the rub

of your body
against the sheen

of silent, big
movements. I

wait for the room
of the room

to hold
a wider table

for our loose need
& the perfect

words,
never spoken.

A VIOLENT SOUND IN ALMOST EVERY PLACE #20

Scattered to the mission,
the thinness of the point,
always sung so lately it

becomes overwrought
with self-sufficient context.
I have chosen to see

what it is like to triumph
despite the person I am.
I have chosen not to join

the chorus, but to sing
quietly, so many songs
that it all becomes one note

slowly raised to live an inch
above my head. When I am
buried, my catalog will be

one inch higher, almost as deep
as my tongue, my throat,
the violent parts of my mind

& it is that context that will
decorate my shoulders
like a soldier that gardened.

A VIOLENT SOUND IN ALMOST EVERY PLACE #22

No sight? It's a maze.
No smell? It's clean
or Indiana. No touch?

It could be hell or love
patient enough to ask.
No sound? It is every

second of heaven, except
for your need to hear
your name said by God.

A VIOLENT SOUND IN ALMOST EVERY PLACE #24

Learn the devotion,
the hunger, hunker

& thirst to be viable
in the eyes of sweet,

beautiful, unspoken love.
I love you, too, but I

know how amazing
it would be for you

to never know how much
or why I decided this.

A VIOLENT SOUND IN ALMOST EVERY PLACE #27

The sky each night is residue, star
spent investigations, with suspects,
so many suspects filling their rings

with circumspection and excusals
of friend, of family, of decent enough
foe. It will be secondhand, the epic

reading of the new world by the first
prophet that asks us for nothing more
than to believe in our own flesh more

than we believe in any holy structure.
He will be glorious and we will hate
him for speaking of such hope without

using a god's name first. When we
start to bury the dead, we will say
only their names and who they loved.

A VIOLENT SOUND IN ALMOST EVERY PLACE #28

I run, always to be
caught. If I ran to be
free, would the rattle

in my knee be less
horror? I can hear
my body all the time,

now. When I try to
scream, my body joins
before my words echo

& the prospect of road
always as the rabbit,
that was, briefly,

a very tight wrinkle.

A VIOLENT SOUND IN ALMOST EVERY PLACE #39

I hold the lope
of your tongue
like a brightening

light, wagging
the rattle of loft
like a full praise

for the muscle
memory of the act.
I am unimpressed.

A VIOLENT SOUND IN ALMOST EVERY PLACE #43

It was right to step
into exploration
with our bodies; it

was the slow language
that saved us more
than the flags did;

but as flesh statues
we were no threat.
The naming sold us

as mapmakers
& we really never
have lived up to that.

A VIOLENT SOUND IN ALMOST EVERY PLACE #45

Light children,
the craft vanishes
between us

& if you have
success with height
& the forgotten

manners of discourse,
swallow the gimmick
& put your mouth

to mine. If our
tongues are calm
we can find

the words to trivialize
the unjust fear
of each other's intent.

A VIOLENT SOUND IN ALMOST EVERY PLACE #53

Show me the eight words on your body.
Show me eight words more that

you want on your body. Those sixteen
words are your blackberry bush

& the rest of what you mean to me,
can be easily parsed through touching.

A VIOLENT SOUND IN ALMOST EVERY PLACE #56

Mostly nest, my weakness
is for the wrong words
& the fondness for their wrong
landing, their battle
& stubborn wish to be more
than just wrong, to be wrongly
profound in their message
of un-interpreted unknown.
I am quiet now, because
this has gotten me in trouble
& there is only so much
I can do about being ornery
& thirty-one at the same time.

A VIOLENT SOUND IN ALMOST EVERY PLACE #57

If I can separate the two halves
of my anxiety,
allow my ego to function
alone by the swimming pool,

while my crippled self folds
mittens into earmuffs, shoves
full programs into my mouth
to avoid the lip quiver

of a raucous crowd. I could
tip the whiskey again,
that would do the trick, that
baby is all strolling ego, that

took my hesitation to stand
next to someone that is yelling
& yelled right back at them,
my words meaningless,

but powerful. I have no bounce
on the pills. I have only fear
off of them. The booze
righted the ship until it drowned

the ship. So, now, I am
a great man, when the rest of you
are quietly behaving. If you yell
at me, I will be your child

& then you'll have to deal
with all of that garbage.
It could be I am writing hundreds
of poems to quiet you down.

A VIOLENT SOUND IN ALMOST EVERY PLACE #58

Absorbed into the field? No.
Rising with it, silently reaching
to kill the moon with resolute

dedication, to be obsession
without proclamation—that is
real flight. When the sun

broaches your fury with a cloud
or two, your instinct will be
to kick dirt at your sister enemy—

do it. Be careful of the good black
all around you, and make sure
you curse without any prostration,

but be violent towards any clear
perception of the tide moving
away from your own home.

A VIOLENT SOUND IN ALMOST EVERY PLACE #59

I salute the loving words,
the good travelers of mine
that always scuttle, rushed

to hyperbole what I meant
after I said what I meant
the way my father would.

I am his son. I have very little
ending for you, but I can
apologize very, very quickly.

A VIOLENT SOUND IN ALMOST EVERY PLACE #60

Ribs
& honey,
my curious
love

of aftermath
is fear
of my cage,
shrinking

to sweet
nothing,
my mind
a candy

in a sea
frothed
to determine
the words

I can no longer
say
with belief.
I believe

the force
of listen,
your world
is not mine

is revelatory,
damning,
a clue of no
more flood.

A VIOLENT SOUND IN ALMOST EVERY PLACE #62

I want, at noon,
one sound
of extreme pain

& the rest
of the hours
I want one sound

of extreme love.
All other minutes
should be silent.

A VIOLENT SOUND IN ALMOST EVERY PLACE #63

No one believes
too much, that we
carry wounds

on our bodies
the same as we
carry wounds

in our bodies
& maybe cancer
is the one connector,

the awfulness
that blesses strength
& weakness equally,

Darren C. Demaree

but really I am talking
about the dinner table
in my childhood

that always was
like cancer, always felt
like a safe place where

only terrible things
could happen.
No one, in our nation

of heat, believes
in a painless world,
but we could watch

our words the way
we watch our bodies.
We could give a damn.

A VIOLENT SOUND IN ALMOST EVERY PLACE #72

Spilling birds, Ohio's fireworks have a song
too delicate for words to be attached to it;

but our brief interaction with each verse
creates a gorgeous desire to be a bird on fire.

A VIOLENT SOUND IN ALMOST EVERY PLACE #75

Forest of sun, I see
how sensual
you can be,

when lost,
I scuttle slowly
around your skirting

urged to be
particular
within your rising

fog. Naked
in late morning,
each flapping wing

means something
tremendous
to a man

looking for any sign
or invitation
to be a creature.

A VIOLENT SOUND IN ALMOST EVERY PLACE #79

Realizing I already had a consciousness without a voice,
I discovered how to sound like a knotted fist, an inhabited
style, without the pursuit of more. I have been very lonely.

Darren C. Demaree

A VIOLENT SOUND IN ALMOST EVERY PLACE #81

It's quiet everywhere else
& the good physics rule
about no information

ever disappearing, not
even in a black hole, that
is discomforting to me now,

as I am hurting today
with no physical burdens
& nothing pressing against

my heart. Those physicists
are still puzzled about a few
things, like dark energy

& if they are willing to slow
my pulse in the everyday,
I will show them dark energy

& explain how it works,
how it drives to destroy me,
even if it never touches matter.

A VIOLENT SOUND IN ALMOST EVERY PLACE #84
for Charles North

Nothing is exceptional, nothing
is the exception, this is a million
feet of mud, and a million feet

of sky littered with odes to birds
& the sound of so many people
& such a tremendous box, that

is what we've got. If my calculations
are right, and they are not close,
I will have to out-loud all of you

& beat my chest without under-
standing what that visual does.
I will learn nothing about my size.

Darren C. Demaree

A VIOLENT SOUND IN ALMOST EVERY PLACE #86

The illusion
is that sound can
be an angel that

saves all of us. No,
words can be
the devil, and when

you shout them
at me, my spine
shivers like hell is

the opposite of what
the artists have shown
it to be. There is real

fire, and that touch
has nothing to do
with your voice

climbing into my pit.
If I had wanted
company here

I would have bought
the book of failed poets
& choked on it.

A VIOLENT SOUND IN ALMOST EVERY PLACE #94
for Steve Kowalski

If we can bundle each other, be comforted
by it, our mouths sharing the sleeplessness
of all keepers, those willing to translate flesh

into a connection of breaths. I would swallow
all anxiety to perch in the planned echoes
of a good friend's speech, the inspiration

of a quiet man, opening his hand to show
the work of good heat, to speak without crying
about the beauty of loneliness abandoned.

Darren C. Demaree

A VIOLENT SOUND IN ALMOST EVERY PLACE #95

I've heard dying, heard its new level
of reality, remarkably ordinary

compared to the nub of gazing
back towards the words of regret.

After I was in the room for the second
body's failing, I found there was less

air in the room when I thought there
would be more. My grandfather

took his air with him, gulped it in
to keep his strength, buried it deep

before we could do the same to him.
I will stutter. I will stammer. My resolve

to speak less, to speak more importantly,
will be abandoned when I die.

And all of the air in my lungs will be left
for my grandson to play with. He will

swim in it, take it for himself, tell
a much better story about my passing.

A VIOLENT SOUND IN ALMOST EVERY PLACE #96
for Farren Stanley

It's a long table—
the starkness
between the intense

and searching,
all of us reaching
out for another

level of reality,
all of us stripped
of reality. I love

poets. I have friends
that are poets.
We all need

such great care.
We all need
the lesson of meta-

phor to be offhand
& present only
in our starling.

Startling caregiver,
consider this blanket
an offering to be more

naked the next time
you chose to be nude. Be
joyful with your intent

Darren C. Demaree

& then when the tide
of refractions washes
you clean, begin again.

A VIOLENT SOUND IN ALMOST EVERY PLACE #97
for Christopher Michel

When it's quiet,
I see the leaves
of your face peel

in the knowledge
of everything
shouted before

you grew deeper,
beyond the warmth
of dispensable fear,

beyond high blood
& helplessness.
When it's quiet,

I see your drifting
spirit as slow tones
of meteor, as rocket

without care of guidance.
I hear your words
amidst this busy space.

A VIOLENT SOUND IN ALMOST EVERY PLACE #98
for John McCormick

If the dark curtain knows best
what splendor is, what gathering
& focus of the all-color can be,

I get the sense that each flap
in the wind is of great importance
to that fabric. It's an inheritance

of two sides. One facing the spark,
the other placed in elegy of the spark.
Gathering, I want to wrap you

around my unstoppable world.
I want to hear the curious things you
have to say about belief in the divine.

Darren C. Demaree

A VIOLENT SOUND IN ALMOST EVERY PLACE #100

There is a village of old blossoms,
which, like a sea finding a river
disperses to the names called, cried

out, *I have one beauty left, and it is
my description of the beauty I once
had.* It is important to listen

to the old names. They keep us
from calling to each other in breaths
that once represented perfection,

it keeps us from giving again the bank
a reed that could catch the wind
& make it music to the arriving seed.

We are precious now, because we are
nothing. What was, and still is true,
has been part of our sound for all time.

A VIOLENT SOUND IN ALMOST EVERY PLACE #104
for David Schloss

Every metaphor has a wish list
& the magisterial waves of ink
always aim for more than one

coastline, but to be a person
on the beach, shirt left behind
in the motel room, waiting to see

where the long drive has brought
you, and it is always a long drive
to an active ocean, can one silk

the saltwater without tasting it?
Covered in the inscriptions of bizarre
timing, I am as much a victim

of the weather as I am a victim
of the fates, but to be given the sense
to know the desert will be dry,

& the mountains are sometimes angry,
that seems to be an inherited pleasure.
If I didn't lose my keys so often,

I would wait in the perfect lean,
in the partial shade, never burning,
lifting my soft tongue, only to be wise.

A VIOLENT SOUND IN ALMOST EVERY PLACE #106
for Zackary Hill

Echoes flock
& disappear
in the almost
shot, never
wounded sky.
And quiet

in our own
coloring, we
could be sky,
too. We could
be given to eyes
& be precious

to the attention
of the indifferent
bastards, holding
their gifts by
the barrel,
always asking

about the burden
of life. Cheap
talk, but other
people dream
only for less pain
& no battle.

If we dream,
we dream
of a good field
& the one cry
every man gets
before his burial.

A VIOLENT SOUND IN ALMOST EVERY PLACE #107
for Mike Grabski

If they are the same flowers,
as if they could be the compression
of an opportunity to dream
of passions beginning in the shit

& the other humorous decorations
of life, I want those fucking flowers
to stay intense, to stay searching
through the garden with all roots.

I want to cheer on the majority
of the beauty that I cannot see
& I want that bloom to be out
of my sightline, because that is belief,

my belief that there is so much stripped
to the nub before I ever see it,
that the whole prayerful vision of things
is all true, a reality too rewarding

to fit inside of me. I want the surprise
& glory of my friends to devastate
the whole scene. I want them to know
before I do, the names of actual joy.

Darren C. Demaree

A VIOLENT SOUND IN ALMOST EVERY PLACE #109

Unique intention,
I want to be silent
& have you know

more because of
my silence, how much
you have endeared

yourself to me. I,
breath over breath
have hurdled all

emotion to be
in stasis, hovering
over your recollection.

Now, tell me
a story. Make it sweet
& about nothing.

A VIOLENT SOUND IN ALMOST EVERY PLACE #116

Unspeaking
& still neon,
why is value

in beauty, verse
without ability,
surrounding

the statues
in a dance
of bounty?

I know some
women
that take art

as a challenge
to become art.
Almost all

of them do it
before the booze
wears off.

Darren C. Demaree

A VIOLENT SOUND IN ALMOST EVERY PLACE #119

The second story is enlightenment.
To me, stimulated to speak out loud,
that need to be more important
than the rest of the room, to perform
without any request, really is insisting
to be a creator. I have come across
these people. Family members, friends
of my wife, parents at the library
with their uncontrollable children,
the one we always call "easily over-
whelmed mother", they all demand
the floor, to tell you about their hardship
& triumph over that hardship.
I give them small responses until the first
story is done, and if they feel comfortable
at the end there is always a throw-away
sentence I love to hear. Smaller even,
a fragment of "I never did love him,
anyway" or "Well, we figured it would be
safer to electrify the fence" or "What
can you do?" Beautiful little reminders
that they're all lost, that they've taken
the stage to show you their lost-ness,
so that if they tell their story, and you
don't call them a monster, then they
are okay. I love these conversations now.
They are worth the pain of the process,
because the second story, the small, injured
one is always filled with understanding
about enlightenment—how far away it is.

A VIOLENT SOUND IN ALMOST EVERY PLACE #122

Shivering owl cry,
blue flame of night
& true vigil of danger,

I appreciate your call
to death, but why does
it feel like your threat

outside my window
can cut my mind
in sleep? Often it is

my best dream you find
tucked in your beak,
bleeding down

your angry, beautiful
throat. Indifferent
elder, be still tonight,

my restlessness
is neither threat nor taste
to your glorious world.

A VIOLENT SOUND IN ALMOST EVERY PLACE #123

Hull of my war, wolf skins
& seasons of roots reaching
for more cover, loud winter

always knows that active
hands are never foreign
to the pointed sounds,

the bleeding that fills all
cavities. My light bones
are warm, weighted by this.

A VIOLENT SOUND IN ALMOST EVERY PLACE #127

A waist covered is the perfect image for a poem,
but the words almost always skin the hip, sharp
to the soul of want, I want to describe, if not first,
then best, how I imagine your hands can witness
the sacrament of removal. If, in my ecstatic state,
I start to wear too many clothes it is because
my roaming has betrayed me, and my wife knows
that I am intensely searching for the right words
to describe another woman's visage. She appreciates
the exercise, but that territory really is all hers
to surprise. On occasion she will wear a wig for me,
but it's the same color hair as hers, the length of play
is surprising, but I am too old not to have a type.

A VIOLENT SOUND IN ALMOST EVERY PLACE #129

Before stone,
the fire burns
the real life

from the bush
& then time
heaps a silence

that can purify
into diamonds
if the corner

of the river
bends correctly,
bends to flow.

A VIOLENT SOUND IN ALMOST EVERY PLACE #130

I can only add to the way things already are,
no, again, what I am saying is that I can only

add to what things are by removing unconscious
shouting, the fathers of our own shouting, the dig

of the tree shoved into our roots. If it is quiet
enough, there can only be things missing?

A VIOLENT SOUND IN ALMOST EVERY PLACE #131

Sourceless fear, I can never see you,
but I always know the direction
in which I hear your creeping, agile

steps. Then, quickly, you are upon me,
with a thousand hands pushing against
my chest, dipping long fingers into

my throat. Friends, if I find it hard to say
I love you in the midst of this creature,
it will not be because I didn't try to

& please take any gagging sounds you hear
from my direction to be an earnest attempt
to put your face in front of this anxiety.

A VIOLENT SOUND IN ALMOST EVERY PLACE #132

The sheen of the wax
from the apple is real
sheen, but beneath
the plastic covering,

the real artist plants
plastic seeds, in hopes
of growing plastic trees.
There are only so many

instruments, and we all
want a garden. We all
want our houses to burn
with the context of garden

to give more meaning
to the blaze. Silent fire,
always looking for walls,
go about your business.

We will find shelter
in the dirt, with the tools
we were given to save us
from the heat of each other.

A VIOLENT SOUND IN ALMOST EVERY PLACE #134

Migration of light across the wall, I have named
each spot you found this morning, given our
yellow box names for each of your galaxies.

It's been hours since I've bought more than belief
from your pattern, and when you finally rested,
just before noon, on the edge of my book shelf,

I took belief in that as well. I named the names
of my favorite poets, thought of their warmth
& anger towards warmth. I told nobody about

my shuffling of alphabetic order into an order
of volume. How powerful was Bob Creeley's
best whisper? I waited for the moon to answer.

A VIOLENT SOUND IN ALMOST EVERY PLACE #136

If you can, sink
the ship back
into the forest,

allow the timber
of your voice
to be tested, held

firm without
seeking, given
root in reserve.

A VIOLENT SOUND IN ALMOST EVERY PLACE #141

Bridges
& some
sundown

by the water,
we expect
explosion

when we see
such beauty,
but in this

world the spark
is there,
the consumption

of the spark
takes place
inside of us.

No sound
is needed,
save for our

appreciation
of the sky
& it's refraction.

Darren C. Demaree

A VIOLENT SOUND IN ALMOST EVERY PLACE #146

The tendency is to yell
& then sleep upon
the reverberations

of our anger, but that
nearness of our tongue
to the hot opening

of our awful mouths,
could that not,
eventually, numb

the entire world, singe
the delicateness
of what began

as a sensual quality?
Picture the fire inside
of you, know the sounds

leaving you forcefully
carry only eventual ash
& no convention of wit.

A VIOLENT SOUND IN ALMOST EVERY PLACE #147

They run like blood,
words with proper
depth, respect

for the movement
& energy required
to believe in them

before you ever say
their meaning. I have
taken old words

& given them names
new to the rest
of the world. They

became mine that way,
they became meaning-
less that way

& when I shout
them, they move only
the hair on your arms.

A VIOLENT SOUND IN ALMOST EVERY PLACE #148

If I could bum an apricot,
feel the odd fruit, allow
my fingers to wrap gently

around the skin of it, push
my teeth to the seed without
ever breaking the breath

of the core, would I then
know the lesson of a keeper?
If I opened my mouth again,

enlightened by the spark
of tender knowledge, would
it matter if I spoke very little?

A VIOLENT SOUND IN ALMOST EVERY PLACE #150

It is not the words
we decay into, it,
the splendid gasses

of reason abandoned
is what we leave
behind in a grave.

If, before that non-
ecstatic state, we
should speak, it will

be, it should be, in
a color we remember
as our own shadow.

A VIOLENT SOUND IN ALMOST EVERY PLACE #152

Urge
& hold
anger
only as

genre
without
heart,
with

stimuli
& tire-
some
crawl.

A VIOLENT SOUND IN ALMOST EVERY PLACE #153

There are no brains in the bell,
but we all stand on our toes
for every song it plays, bursting

with surprise that the sounds
from the tower have found us,
alerted us to the tide of flawless

time. If we wrapped our arms
around the metal, around
the composite, the mixed-media

of the construction of the bell,
would that be enlightenment?
No. We would feel even smaller

& would grow to hate
the obnoxious sound, repeating
too close to the mechanics

of the heart, a song so simple,
an answer so vague, that we'd believe
the elemental projection too awful

to be a calling for anything dynamic.

A VIOLENT SOUND IN ALMOST EVERY PLACE #157
for Erin Elizabeth Smith

Merely
& the needling,
the rapid

meekness
is fog on a paddle
boat ride,

but dear, oh dear
I asked you
to be whole

with the calm
waters, because
I thought

the electricity
from the sky
would give you

more life,
I thought
if you had fear

that was
un-definable
your song

would save us
from living
in the beyond.

A VIOLENT SOUND IN ALMOST EVERY PLACE #158
for Jeff Zbaeren

Decoy your individual,
men, look strong
& be stronger

when your name
has no skin, come across
as an ocean without shore

& use your salt to carry
the rest of the life around
your flawed, burly nature.

When a light tongue
says your name three times,
give her your voice

& your shoulders. Use
the rest of your arms
to curry enlightenment.

Raise your voice one time
before you die, do it, men,
in praise of a stranger

attempting to do what
you did. You were tide.
You loved a vague moon.

A VIOLENT SOUND IN ALMOST EVERY PLACE #161

I appreciate the risks of the postcard—the lovely,
inexact gesture of mailing one place to another
in a braggart's way of meditation on not being home

& tonight will be flawless without you here with us
& it is only that reason—your absence—that we have
included you in our trip. Please, remind us to keep

you at this distance when we return home. Your voice
rises to interact with our pleasure in a way that slips,
lessens our ecstatic state. I should stop sending these.

A VIOLENT SOUND IN ALMOST EVERY PLACE #163

Wrists roll in the throat, wring
the balance from your eloquent
concept of never touching borders

of another person's harmony,
and then somebody's hands have
the last everything bagel

& your impression of the world
is one where we kill for water,
for flour, for sesame seeds?

A VIOLENT SOUND IN ALMOST EVERY PLACE #167

Spill the birds
onto the ice,

the one that rolls
& flies before

reaction constructs
into meaning

& real death,
that bastard

is enlightenment
we have a name for.

A VIOLENT SOUND IN ALMOST EVERY PLACE #168

If we gather at the ending,
near the brisk eye
that never gathers the grey

will we be able to pick one
sharp color to flag the memorial
of our dark, animal losses?

Before we knead our thighs
& rename the communions,
let us all agree that if we shout

a name towards the naked
branches it should be a woman's
& if we whisper anything

to the roots hidden beneath
the blood, hidden with our
sense of dirt, it should

be remorseful. We should be
willing to give the whole tree
a stillness. We never will.

Darren C. Demaree

A VIOLENT SOUND IN ALMOST EVERY PLACE #170

Spoken to be caught
in each utterance,
I have strapped black
leather to my precious
breath. I have given heat
to the hides, mid-
utterance I have flown
with many names
of pilots folded under
my tongue. This has all
been aimless ritual,
but if my bones are hollow
it is because I believed
they could be just that.

A VIOLENT SOUND IN ALMOST EVERY PLACE #178

Maple
to sleep,

the caring
cardboard

collects
the relics

born to post-
beauty

& I bag
the yard

to movie
soundtracks

where the hero
gets to watch

death stretch
to mock

the speed
we claim.

He always
dies in color

Darren C. Demaree

these days,
tremendous

black stems,
leaking red.

A VIOLENT SOUND IN ALMOST EVERY PLACE #180

It's harmful, the medicine
of catharsis, the twist
& appeal to become whole

by taking pieces
from another person's boundary
& making vivid the harsh

failings they lump against
the ankle to limp. Once wronged,
once defiant, you can become bits

tremendous in aim,
but to be a whole track again,
hoping for passengers,

hoping for fresh joy—that could be
the wrong surprise for everyone
& remove a bridge to the unheard.

A VIOLENT SOUND IN ALMOST EVERY PLACE #184

Shackled to the drifting,
the angle of never arriving,

I would trash myself
for momentum

before I ever screamed
to gather a sorrowful tide

of faint responses. Vigor

for vigor, if you want life
& the adrenaline of gesture

to be more than wind
in the grasses, you will need

to resist the urge
to weep without scarring

your passing devices,
your passengers,

your surrounding air,
which will suspect you

from the beginning,
of heated resurrections.

If you set the boat on fire,
be prepared to surf the dead.

A VIOLENT SOUND IN ALMOST EVERY PLACE #185

If it was all consequence, we would hear
the shovel's migration every morning
& when the moon withered into day
it would join the sunken in communion
with garments of yesterday. Rummaging
for the bushes that could burn me up,
I have felt punishment to be random
& awfully vague for the things I've done.
I've told a lot of people, in hopes that they
would punish me for my past behavior
& they seem steady with the future
the way I will never become about the past.
I remain guilty, granting sins to each
languid passerby. They, too, have songs
to sing, they appear to be muttering.
I speak clearly, without regard for myself
& there appears to be little interest in a mob.

A VIOLENT SOUND IN ALMOST EVERY PLACE #186

My silence
is more arrogant
than your detonator

& if we become ash,
sentimental
at the doorway

of imagining outcomes,
I will avoid your death
with my smug tongue

wagging the alphabet.
the same way
I learned cunnilingus.

Like then,
this posturing
will give us no action

& no voice,
other than the threat
of peeling slowly away.

A VIOLENT SOUND IN ALMOST EVERY PLACE #189

If I carry my window
by the wooden frame,
march with the fragment

of my wall through
the hyphenates of town,
always leaning against glass,

always sanding the dark
maple with my harsh hands
& I were stopped

by the sound of breaking
glass, I would have to assume
that destruction

is taking place outside
of my home. My trail
would be silent. My trail

would be telling of what
it is like to ground a comet
& drag that business

past two Wendy's
before you reach Broadway,
before the fire starts again.

It is a play if we are looking
out at it. It would be our lives
if I dropped the act,

if I responded to the burning
shrapnel attached to my name
with more than an abstraction.

A VIOLENT SOUND IN ALMOST EVERY PLACE #190

I want to bury
my father's voice
& I want to be
graveside, vigilant
to the sorrowful,
plummeting act
of waiting to hear
him speak again.

When I was a boy
I wanted to un-bury
his voice, because
it was the silence
that was killing me,
the thorough thought
process that gave
holes for us to stay in,
un-fed, un-loved,
wretched, fouled
by our mistakes
& our weakening
mother, who spoke
only in cautions.

I want to bury
my father's voice
& I want the kind
things his age
has given us, his
own fear of death
has given us
to be his last words.

Darren C. Demaree

A VIOLENT SOUND IN ALMOST EVERY PLACE #196

Flesh as a target, my nearness
to the hunters, the shipwrecks
& the last stage of pseudo-
intelligentsia has me quiet,
saying nothing, allowing the
debris that is those people
to haggle over whether or not
their persimmon & barley
soup is better with a rock in it
or ham in it, or whether or not
the Super Bowl is a garish,
masturbatory spectacle, devoid
of all that humanity could be
& really I have nothing to say
to anything of that. I want
those people to put their heads
down, exhausted by their wagging,
so I can eat my sandwich w/ chips
& watch the game without a rattle
of judgment about the lowering
state of America, what artists
are doing by exposing themselves
to such a dance. If I leave salt
around my couch, will I be safe?

A VIOLENT SOUND IN ALMOST EVERY PLACE #198

You cannot wing a bone
that rattles loose

& chased by wet finger-
tips, curved to bloom

through the thistle,
the fantasy and horror

of garden at night.
If I raise my voice so near

a fountain, with a statue
built for the dead spitting

& re-spitting water,
will his granite echo

my words, give them cement,
weight that will push

past the vines
of our floral company?

Two bare feet
on a tremendous moss,

I am standing steady
with my heart full

of dark green memorial,
I am speaking,

without catharsis,
to give pool to my guests.

A VIOLENT SOUND IN ALMOST EVERY PLACE #200

If my tongue is a bearing beam,
surely all that wagging will bury
the mine without survivors,

with the last pit pony drowning
in the discovery of meaningless
weight. There might be poems

underneath the crushed light bulbs
of the tunnel, but can you tell me if
this industry is one of any profit?

A VIOLENT SOUND IN ALMOST EVERY PLACE #203

If I am to get rich off of the words
unspoken, I will probably need
to learn how to draw naked girls

with a depth of scenery
that does nothing for the imagination.
Gorgeous hangings, the trick

will be to roll inexcusably
with the inscriptions of gathering
times. Metaphor will be useless.

A VIOLENT SOUND IN ALMOST EVERY PLACE #207

If we can carry the burst, the devouring
sentiment that inches down to the relationship
between drowning and being made to drown,

will we have a great trouble breathing
with so many of our machinations bent
on choking our actions with the full confetti

of epigrams? My words are crucially important
to me, but if they try to sneak their way into
your cavities without permission, fight them off

& we can share the burial of my subroutine,
we can grant the dance of silence to everything
I do. I will need a new hat, then, to show emotion,

but the rattle of my wrists will become boulders
nearby for the lightness of empty air to decorate.
It will be quieter. It will be peaceful, without harm.

Darren C. Demaree

A VIOLENT SOUND IN ALMOST EVERY PLACE #208

I believe in the language of salvation.
I believe that language loses certainty
with each decibel it rises. I believe

any sound that shakes the ground
is too dynamic to carry another person
& that realization could save everybody,

could save non-believers, could create
a beautiful unease in every bully's gullet.
I believe it matters if you cross the river

& it matters less if you can describe
in great detail the ecstatic state you felt
when you reached the waiting arms

of someone who cannot describe
that feeling either. If we must use words
to give faith, can we make them inexact

& quiet? Can we make those words
the symbol for radical, inclusive searching?
Can I tell you a secret? Can I whisper it?

A VIOLENT SOUND IN ALMOST EVERY PLACE #210

The ribbon of your great, lonesome
ability to be a giant, stomping through
the valley with your tremendous voice,

burying, re-planting humanity beneath
previous burials, mounds of spirit
ground into dust again by your thrusting

tongue. You have arrived at my cheek
with no more than a trail of spittle.
If you had more than volume

& the shuttle-shake of a modern prophet,
bent to out-shout the rattle of progress,
I would listen. I would be tender

with your words, the way I expect you
to be tender with mine. I am not afraid
that the people will hear your voice

over mine. I am petrified by the thought
that what you are saying will waste the tide
we've spent years culling from the cosmos.

WE ARE ARROWS

WE ARE ARROWS #1

There are no holes, even a black hole is poorly named, because what it really has become is a black door with another reality waiting on the other side of it.

There are no wholes, we have put our fingers in everything, we have tasted the wound, we have named it so we could remember the taste, and that perhaps is the most human thing about us.

There are no holes, even the seeds rest upon something, get covered by something, grow past something, reach to crop for something.

There are no wholes, though the most complete stars are firmament, are mathematics, the numbers tracking how often we touch without knowing we are touching.

There are no holes, but there is so much matter pierced and growing though the piercing, that we believe there is a webbing, that we are trapped here, that we might not be the main attraction.

There are no wholes, there are no pure colors that we haven't created either, and that vagueness is the heat we taste on each other's breath; it is the vigor that allows us to be lightning among the many clouds.

WE ARE ARROWS #2

The sheets are warmth. We are lithe; we are not busted in presentation.

If in retrospect, you saw us diving in flight, it was the wind shaking us, as we are not with the wind.

We are arrows that began with the muscles of a uniquely driven animal that lives four stories in four realities at all times.

The sheets are warmth the same way the desert is warmth.

It is not cruel for us to find the shoulder blades of this world, and plunge through to another world, in fact we talk about leaving our bodies to do this all of the time.

WE ARE ARROWS #3

Resemblances sprawl the cancer, display the rot we run for, always running for, and at rest there are so many places we could never have faith in because we passed them without a result.

Intended to die, we have made whole lives about changing the question, about coming up with a new question that never ends in questioning.

I want to be born again, not so I can be alive longer, but so I can spend less time explaining myself to those I love so much that I am willing to forgive their quick deaths, willing to celebrate the sweaty processional without the landmark of a finish line.

WE ARE ARROWS #7

Raced to the bulb, the husbandry of strange flesh angled to the ground, always angled to the ground, never planted willingly near the plead to be imprisoned and free forever.

You want to die.

Of course you do.

It will take a great deal of injury to garner such confession, and rightly so.

We are more telling when we have no threat, and I am telling you that you are right to be stubborn in this life, and when out of you the river finds a sea to join, when you lose half of what you were in a split second, what hangs on will have to be weighed down, sunk to never rise again.

That fight is my favorite thing about you.

WE ARE ARROWS #8

Vulnerable without
action, we have lost
too much blood to
vibrate only in the
marrow.
    Offered
as an integral piece,
offered as a toy, we
have thrust both feet
into the mouth of the
ground, lit the small
fat in our bottom lip
on fire, and recited
our demands like
they are prayers to
a flush desert.
    So full of chances
to tongue the eyes
of every photograph
of every combustion
of every lover, we
hinge each grain
against another grain,
and as the wave
develops we learn
again how shakable
a singular flower can
be.

Sign of no
shadow, we are never
lonely, we are direct
in our belief that the
sun above us is
waiting for a good
dance to frame
the next mountain.

WE ARE ARROWS #9

I have struggled with the bells, the towers
we have built to surround them, and I
have struggled without a sentimental cloud
emerging from each ring.

I want to be sincere about my faith in my
own people, but to light the fireworks next to
the houses of god, has turned my love for you
into theater.
I am comfortable being spectacle, if you are
comfortable having no other name than your
own.

WE ARE ARROWS #15

Intractable twilight, I was thinking of such flux while watching the thread of water peek out from the frozen creek in the ravine.

Darkened to the daughter of each season, everything, all the time, feels like it will never end.

It will all end in faith, if we believe first that our water is the first gauge of how we treat the ghosts of real tide.

Once, with good strength, I saved a drowning child, and I have done nothing like that since.

I am still the man that saved the drowning child, though my strength, my width and belief that the water gave me the child to save, has sank back into the rocks.

WE ARE ARROWS #17

Hip lick, I target the curiouser trampoline, the entwine that delivers the feeling of revolution without any following changes.

I want, at times, to know we are not precious to each other, and I want to know that this feeling is misleading me to a recoverable place.

WE ARE ARROWS #20

Unfenced, we have imagined wrongly that every cornfield contains a proper ghost.

Every cornfield has a body in it.

Not all of those bodies could maintain such spirit next to the quiet of a state route.

WE ARE ARROWS #24

It's the tracing, the outline of our fists that never allow for an extension of our good temptation, to raise all fingers and deliver any opportunity to any approximate bonding.

We wanted to be remembered far tougher than we ever were.

We wanted to be controlled, outlandish in our wrestling with the statues of the past.

The artist should have paused over our bellies, taken molds of them, tickled us a bit.

That reaction is our best reaction.

WE ARE ARROWS #25

Dangled obedience, our flesh, the hinges of our flesh, the adult of our flesh, has enough history to plunge, compounded by our exertions to be a bird, to hunt the sun, the worm, the opened skins of our grounded contemporaries.

I want most of all to find the momentum of gravity, to become planted, face first, into the ribcage of a finch, to nestle inside the torn wings of it, to rename it whatever I please.

This is why we have saved flight for machines.

This is why all birds know their taste for innards does little to make them special.

WE ARE ARROWS #28

Abundant collars, sometimes we are so far from any garden, that any blood found near that nakedness, must have come from the other animals.

We have hot convulsions, daily, we have cyclone motions beneath our own skin, but with that rise our own flush will rise only to a hiding spot.

It is wasteful to be such a tremendous physical spirit, and to be all of the signs of a god, but none of the abandon it would require.

WE ARE ARROWS #33

I understand the forest is for burials.

We need more forest.

The narrow rows will hold us together for a long time, and when we are uncovered by the wolves, they will recognize our devotion to them by our willingness to be gifts for them.

We need more forest.

From the sky it will appear as if our gestural nature granted sacrifice before it ever granted pleasure.

It will be a glorious misleading.

WE ARE ARROWS #46

Our fingers do not peck the dirt.

We are searching the dark fringe of life for berries, we are squeezing everything, we are tasting everything.

The shower of dirt does nothing to protect us from the sun.

Two hands full, dumping time and pursuit with religious ferocity, belief that each action is a reaction to the creep of the tide.

Our fingers do not peck the dirt.

We don't have that kind of river, the kind that shows the rhythm and then shows it again.

WE ARE ARROWS #48

Rank the lessons of the whispering curb of humanity, our raised moment, acknowledged to the landing of the heel.

Gravity granted, we should land our only step on the ball of our toes.

That is ego.

We should have more ego about this.

WE ARE ARROWS #49

For one point, a full beat, the indent before the puncture, it feels like being chosen by God, like the splitting skin (before the blood) is an acceptance of such glory.

We have many scars that bear witness.

We have held fast that the blood is a celebration.

We have seen the buckets, culled and rung from embattled rags, their spilling sway a demonstration, a response to our beliefs.

For one point, a full beat, we needed to know why our flesh could flood the scene without any rain, and we learned quickly how much weakness that really was.

WE ARE ARROWS #50

It is like light, the almond held in the moon's frame, and still there is an outline of humanity in the nut that even the tides cannot distract us from.

We see our own faces, greatly defined, in the thighs of each other.

When we see each other in great protein, in a great conductor, in the veil behind the veil behind the veil of the sun.

All we ever see is a reflection of good nature, and our lack of shoulders in the process.

WE ARE ARROWS #53

The torn, the entire instrument of cellular breaking, is that not the most promising of music?

The mending is always huddled, quiet, the tending trances we all develop behind darkened doors that can maintain almost everything.

Those songs are hymn.

The destruction of those songs is hymn.

Any song, sang with any belief is hymn.

Grand actions of my heart, they begin always with the torched path, the small longing of the first divide, that took place a millennia ago.

I have a wife, I have a family, it will be their hands that finally put me back together, and they will do so silently.

WE ARE ARROWS #55

Prize of self, first certainty of a fat sprawl, we afforded a hinge between this world and the next because we needed to understand the mechanics of such things.

We love our shadows.

We dance to see the fold of our time dance against the wall, the sidewalk, and we lament the loss of that small connection of ourselves.

Very little of this world is hidden, what makes us think that when we disappear there is a possibility that we will reappear somewhere else?

If we are all children, shouldn't we already know that our shadows can go nowhere without our height, our mortal wiggle.

WE ARE ARROWS #58

Tug of passion, the peace has given us the elbow room to want so badly we would war for completion.

We are predictable animals.

We are never cold for long.

Sometimes, our lust comes dipped in blood, and that warmth comes with many names.

WE ARE ARROWS #59

Burnished air, measured for a thick suit of humanity, our strangeness and the height of our strangeness are quickly becoming the same thing.
We can fly.
    We don't always land where we should.
    We can fly.
    We don't know yet how to land in a field the way a ghost does.
    We can fly.
    The cracked slate has kept track of our violent landings.
    We can fly.
    The memories of that flight are kept by everything.

WE ARE ARROWS #60

Enormous black, a clearing at night can become a great longing, free of all fear, if you know how comforting one fire can become.
    The eventual truth will look like fireworks.

WE ARE ARROWS #61

I was worried for a long time about the hinge and signs of failure, that at some point I would just be put down, as in buried with breath beneath the question marks of my own person, that since I had no answers to the sustainable questions, I deserved to be cast below the root systems.

We are all worried there might be hell.
We are all worried about the evaluations of the sky and those that carry us.

I was worried for a long time, and then I wasn't worried at all, as I came to terms with the lack of ultimate answers.

My real life began when I created my own questions.

WE ARE ARROWS #62

Knotted semblance, I swallowed the un-blessings with good displacements for fire of each page of each memory.

We are rope.

We wish we were oak.

We burn well, so close to an old sun, that has never bothered to forget that we are also talismans for each other.

Pulled to repetition, our dance sometimes, appears to be in time with a song nobody can hear.

WE ARE ARROWS #66

for Bill Cohen

Radiating the good hazard, the floating desire
to be pinned upon what we have first imagined
as a powerful feeling, we have stenciled this
against our skins as a possible flood to raise us
all and minimize the mountain's clout.

The execution has given us the intricacies
of regret for the lost, the drowned, the best
painters.

Sharpened by the rendering, a man that
stands with his heels against the riverbank, will
know the best truth of our lungs' capabilities,
will disregard them completely in the invention
of his own swimming stroke.

WE ARE ARROWS #71

We have allegiances to the swollen feelings, but
those feelings in flight give the worst wiggle to
trace against the sun, the worst entry into the
scene of action. Almost all swollen feelings
lead to rolling around in the mud.

Almost all swollen feelings find themselves
buried in a blood count.

WE ARE ARROWS #72

Sneer to stray, the aurora is cloaked in arrowheads, scattered in the multiples that rain down upon the bright specialty of hope.

There is a shimmer to every heaven.

This is why we are so drawn to silver, drawn to sugar, drawn to the trail of sweat that can create, can radiate belief in practically any cloud.

WE ARE ARROWS #75

Thick medium, our maturity has led us to the essential bridges.

It was our bodies that decided first we could fly from here, we could land in paradise without increasing our strength, without ever knowing how the wind wanted so badly to tease us, to bury us in the tides above the ocean.

We are suspended, most of all, in our desire to take off from the world, and our contradictory desire to live amongst the planted people we love so whole-heartedly.

WE ARE ARROWS #81

Rock against our cheeks, we are tremendous
beings when we first acknowledge our warmth
is warmth to all things.

WE ARE ARROWS #82

Stern grease, the swipe to keep the course
slipping in profundity is a verbal feast for the
volume of a bone grinding upon another bone.
This is not entertainment.
This is the emotional response to the
sternness of physics.

WE ARE ARROWS #83

Refuse the mildness of the courtyard.
If it is dark where you land, the light could
bring you anything.
It could be incredibly brilliant to experience
more than relief.

WE ARE ARROWS #84

If we begin with descent, how much stillness
becomes the blade waiting to own the segments
of our shadow?
Shake, damn you, shake.

WE ARE ARROWS #91

The lilac bursts in eventual truth, that the bagging of cut grass blades has nothing to do with the lilac, but it is a lick from our blade that keeps the flowering of fear whole.

All beauty is in the same danger as an overgrown lawn.

All last looks at beauty are taken by the deciding edge, the awfulness of rampant care that is pushed by the deadliest of momentum, hate and jealousy.

WE ARE ARROWS #93

We are accidentally alive.

Thrown to the weeds and privileged to be cold, never astonished, we are ferocious as this night rises, we are in full stimulus with what the moon could do to us if we joined the ocean willingly.

We are accidentally alive.

We are the storm electric to the touch of anything, and when that risk is upon us all three shudders can collapse fear into vibration, vibration into action, action into grace.

We are accidentally alive, we are so much more and so much less than an ornament, and we are profoundly determined to fill this entire void.

We are the sheared and the shearing of this universe.

WE ARE ARROWS #94

For Billy Simms

Cracked empires, it is those missing pieces that can best take us in, make us whole, give us direction when submission is no longer an option.

Even feathers can appear to be strong in the right fists.

Even the spasmodically charmed devils still need to look at the clouds and see more than anger or the absence of anger.

When it comes to saving, I want to be close to those people desperate to be saved by no one.

I want hands that resemble blocks of wood.

I want to imagine they see my face when they see nothing at all.

I want to know men entitled to be visible from any height.

WE ARE ARROWS #95

For Laura Beattie

The great distance rushes past any black-eyed elegy of separation; it rushes to harm only the carefully trimmed idea of how approximate affection needs to be to add pieces of the puzzle of our daily lives.

We are always doing our best to blow out the fires that can close any land.

We are always doing our best to celebrate a return home without any sadness that they once left at the start.

Bless the mornings when we feel whole feelings toward anyone.

Bless the smoke on the map that when squinted upon, fools us into thinking it is only one hand length from our shoulders to yours.

WE ARE ARROWS #100

Not yet poisoned, we are wind-aided, our pitched cries never dragging in the fields or our wrenched church houses.

Every building we can see from this height looks like a church.

Everything communal, when speeding overhead, appears to be a church.

Entrance from the level of the door sullies almost all hope.

We spend most of our time, waiting to be thrown again towards the sun, towards the strange, wonderful distance flight provides.

Distance can convince us of almost anything.

WE ARE ARROWS #109
For Steve Kowalski

Jaws and the conflicting fountains of decadence behind them, we should first be judged by the look in our eye; we should first be tight to the spine so that we can outline our best curve among the approaching, warring waters.

Water can't hate other water.

Water rushing into other water becomes the same force, pooling to rush again.

We would best be served, by serving each other lean love, by separating our teeth just wide enough to sneak out the intention to be reasonless with our hearts, to be sure that our sharpest tooth is never used.

WE ARE ARROWS #110
For Daisy Levy

Greased, streaked across our breasts, there is no valley for good blood that rises, heaps itself into an intractable study of scooping gestures, of lowering to raise the other blood as well.

Persuasion is never an ornament.

Persuasion can take what is forged deepest amongst us, our original targets, and suggest abandoning the violence of our small flight.

We are always shy of being alone, and that is mostly because we find others to become precious weapons for, others that were never weapons to begin with.

Some of us are born to radiate the humility of a steady path to the mountain's peak.

Some of us are that peak.

WE ARE ARROWS #112

Even the ghost of a bloom, shot through, torn or thrown to the ground, filled with the gravel that can lead to a garden, stands rarely to be shot through again.

Our best efforts should thicken the middle of beauty; but too often we find ourselves trimming the edges, searching for a way in, without destruction.

To acknowledge beauty is to press your own print into the hinge of it; but to refuse the gift of it, would surely remove us from the garden entirely.

WE ARE ARROWS #113

I reply to the mildness more and more, treat it as danger done up to appear like the rest of us.

Several steps from any sheen, we grow to want the danger we stumbled upon in our youth.

We were stupid and we can be stupid again, but how many of us can take such a shearing without losing our heads?

WE ARE ARROWS #118

Around the back, it appears sometimes as if our ribs are reaching past our arms, moaning to be the spread of wings, to be in flight.
We were never angels.

We were never birds; but that feeling remains, that we can take the valuable nature of flight and cash in again on our inventive spirit, reach past the fields with our own chest's movement.

We have given up gluing feathers to our arms, but when the good blood rises and our eyes go oval with the adrenaline, we will believe our power to be limitless.

We were never angels.

We were never birds.

We have been mad inventors for all of time.

WE ARE ARROWS #122

Every water, full of all age and sorrow, has a bottom, an easy silt to search through.

We can not say as much about the hope and drive of the sky.

'Out of our reach' still means the heavens or tough physics, and that sort of magic keeps us planted here, looking up at all times.
Every water means drowning.

Every cloud gives lightning more meaning.

WE ARE ARROWS #123

Spun to bobble the entry point, we have finally gotten past our relationship with ash trays, have traded them in for real fires or the sidewalk, have given them our nostalgia and a partial lung, but never so much of our voice.

We, trimmed to maturity, could be mistaken for a tree, if we are driven deep enough into the ground that our sharp, metal bits become hidden by nature.

Our first inclination was to burn everything, and that idea was so close to starting over that it made sense.

Now, when we smoke, we know it means celebration of our continued battles with the core of our own bodies.

Now, we know it is only a personal threat.

WE ARE ARROWS #125

Folds, rowed to visible extension, we have come to believe in only what we can exercise into un-belief, into what we can train to become nothing when we need to hide it most of all.

I believe the sinking springs of prostration should be reserved for strangers.

I believe we all believe that waterfalls are nature's great tease of spirit.

If only we could all feel the rush and allow the parting of our own waters for any valued stranger.

I love my family, but I could, with my full heart, love you even more.

WE ARE ARROWS #128

Boldly alive, our un-sharpening becomes invitations to be alive near the exact folds of another person's un-sharpening.

It will be incredibly beautiful, with all of our blood accumulating beneath the skin, never ready to leave more than a tender bruising.

We have greatly under-valued the thick pressure of each other's weight, the flushness of our skins could be the dull saving we need to become more than arrows.

WE ARE ARROWS #130

Berry-warm, circled by blossoms, was there any doubt that every version of every picture of Eden looked like a target?

Stardust or rib bone, the care of this strong, rolling orb, welcomed our singing as hymn, gave us our first god, nature's whole design.

We are predictably drawn to be understanding of temptation's first overture, but what comes after our acceptance of a plunging accord, has fueled the real debates ever since.

WE ARE ARROWS #131

The translation of energy is a different humility, as we wonder aloud about the slamming radiation of what can push us towards each other or erase the myths of the sequence of the lord.

We are a vehicle as much as we are a direction.

We are forged near the sun, then held at a great distance from our father.

We are the best of hot sands, filtering into the ornery rivers of our dedicated surroundings.

Happy-hearted, we have arrived alive and courageous in the mouth of our own developing tongues.

WE ARE ARROWS #132

Off the plant, the field can fill our surrender
with the torn-up blooms of a full belly.
It is no matter to the story how long it takes
to wrap ropes around our own bodies, but what
shapes us all is how much battle we can do with
a full belly.
We do not need to be hungry to rip each
other to pieces.
We do not need to have our mouths open in
case it should rain glory into our caverns.
We cannot arrive fast enough at the decision
to eat what we need, to speak very little about
anything, and to share the liberties of our last
looks at each other without a single moment of
pain.

WE ARE ARROWS #135

It's real. It grows almost everywhere.
It's real.
It's the vivid limb of our challenge, to be
more than a collection of angry, pointed
munitions, to be soft, to be alive and in the
good trance of humanity.
It's real.
We are real.
We are metal and careful design.
We are the feathers that guide us as well.

WE ARE ARROWS #136

Of space and the burden of immensity, what does it matter to one branch, if it never understands the root system?

How many drops of water does it take for you to know that rain, almost always, is good care?

Two arms raised to reach into the astrological pudding will only make you sticky, but then again, some of us don't mind the sweet muck of such experiences.

If a tree can grow out of the side of a mountain, then there is no force that we should fear.

WE ARE ARROWS #139

If it must be a clean break from the licking scoundrels of our exuberant splashes in the rivers of America, then how best should we celebrate the gambling spirit we first established with our bodies?

We learned to gamble our extensions before we learned to gamble our core, but that has never been too far from the banks of our decency.

This is how traveling began—not to see other places, but to show other waters the entirety of our bodies.

The nudity is perhaps the best thing about us.

WE ARE ARROWS #140

It's a soft socket—the way we fit here, so near the indescribable hum that our translations give us narrative to the waiting.

There will be a spectacle.

There will be fireworks that shoot around your ripeness.

We could be, in the end, an epic intricacy of the first carnival.

WE ARE ARROWS #148

Pull the belt against the grain of the wood.

What raises with such punishment is what will work best in our magnificent sequencing of pain that can be strung like garland or a cheap necklace in our most public of rooms.

We all love trees, stripped by process, mangled into display or boat.

We all love trees, unflinching trees, that never give up the knot, that make everything harder for us.

Pull the belt against the grain of the wood, if you have good leather it will be your arms that give up first.

We will let arms hang from almost anything.

WE ARE ARROWS #150

We are countlessness.

We are counted incorrectly.

We are named, and so we believe in language.

We are named by numbers, and so science is both hinge and door to us.

We are countlessness, because we are not a blackberry and we are not a stone.

We are something beautiful and awful.

We are the formula for almost everything that has no answer.

We are the buoy only for chaos in an ocean too tremendous to have any understandable moniker.

We are a sign of no comfort.

WE ARE ARROWS #152

If loneliness is an oven, then love is freedom. Love is choosing not to be only freedom. Love is quick to find the essential in the open spaces, because dancing, dammit, is an act of the lovely and the unlovely people that need room to kick things, even if those things are sometimes each other.

We always begin surrounded.

We always end surrounded.

If in the middle, the surrounding starts to panic you, then love, I suppose, could be an oven as well.

If loneliness is an oven, then love is freedom.

Loneliness is a freedom too, one that never ends.

Loneliness is the most awful surrounding of all.

WE ARE ARROWS #156

Metal on skin, we have no translation for the shifting focus of that flush contact.

Disappearing back into what will never be more valuable than the brewing of a cup of coffee, we should value the other metal far less than we value even the worst of human skin.

If only we weren't so afraid of each other's greases, the holding plank of our cupped hands would be filled with I was, I am, we shall all be worth the stretching of our tendons.

WE ARE ARROWS #159

Feathers and the petal-tissue, the rest of art can be the rest of life if we find the muscle behind the fluff.

I have come to bury flowers just deep enough in the garden that can be picked by my children.

I have buried money all over my property.

Now, with the gentleness set aside for the ones I love, and the glint distracting the rest of you fuckers, I can get some work done.

WE ARE ARROWS #160

The heart eats the blossom because the heart wants so deeply to be a blossom.

The heart is not a blossom.

The heart is root to our great howling, and without that sound we would be stem and loon, we would be the possibility of strength, but no more.

WE ARE ARROWS #168

The meadow is a dark ceiling, and when the lid closes the anywhere and anytime to right here and right now, even the rabbits become an unimaginable horror.

We are inseparable from our fear that this is our only world.

We should get over that.

We should celebrate it with great care.

WE ARE ARROWS #172

Whether it is the look of the folding truth, bending us to acceptance or the willingness of all humans to be taken if it might mean being taken somewhere else, the exuberance of our wait appears aimed at weakening our own hearts.

Have you seen a wild horse tear through this world?

Have you felt that jealousy overwhelm you, drown your instinct to name things away from your own action?

Have you found comfort, yet, in releasing your own animal upon the rolling countryside?

We are constructions—that does not mean we weren't built to confound our constructs.

WE ARE ARROWS #176

Spelled to scatter, we have cracked the grain with our teeth, spilled it into our gullets.

I have had many dreams about becoming the field, being the field, having that kind of growth begin inside of me, and ultimately giving it away without any name.

I have not thought much about the consequences of those expectations.

I have thought even less about the possibility of being fallow.

Now, with that thought piercing all other thoughts, I can think of nothing else.

WE ARE ARROWS #177

Gorged and insignificant, our raw dances become lopsided theory as their anchor remains in our strange flesh and the witnesses of this process become ghosts twice as fast as any rehearsed display.

We are excellent without witnesses.

We are entertaining as fuck.

We are coming closer and closer to never being alone again.

That flushness will redefine even our most simple ability to be originally embarrassing.

We could lament this most of all.

WE ARE ARROWS #178

We are lightning bolts.

We can't worry about being spent.
Our energy was in the arrival.

We are already spent, and yet our coil remains vibrant.

On a hot night, we can hold our flesh to the sky and be written again without error.

We are lightning bolts.

We can't worry about being spent.

WE ARE ARROWS #185

Pinched to dedication, our kisses present the proper tension between bodies, how quickly it can fade to consumption when our blood rises to the level of the invisible master.
The science of why we penetrate each other at all is fascinating.

The science of our folding in again, of the severity of our desire to move recklessly, to clash against the other, identifiable atoms, relation of our most base relation, is truly fireworks.

WE ARE ARROWS #190

If we are looking for safety amongst the plums and danger between the crocodile's eyes, then we have lost the territorial guidelines and the million cuts on our forearms will turn into waterfalls and the only sated beast will be the degrees of the danger that led to our swallowing.

The degrees in which we are completely safe exist somewhere between the fruit and the heavens.

If you have a taste for heaven, then you have a taste for crocodile as well.

If you can taste the chili powder in the chocolate, then your body will assume that every cloud is different, that wings are for birds, that we run only to work our coast of possibilities.

WE ARE ARROWS #193

We might be lost, but we are never directionless.

Sometimes, we escort the animal.

Sometimes, we escort the person with the animal's head.

Sometimes, we might wheelbarrow an empty white dress to the closest body of water.

Sometimes, we are dragged by the animal we first escorted, as is the custom of good parties.

We might be lost, but we are never directionless.

We are constant in our pursuit of differing shades of company, but we can agree that every exchange increases the possibility of being drowned.

Never together, never alone, we are in parade, in full demonstration of a worn path where our bodies are the most limitless decorations.

WE ARE ARROWS #195

Segmented fruit, we have arrived in stages, we have entered with a piercing action, without sound, without regret for the minimalist thwack of our descent.

We have no existence until we acknowledge the width of our own shoulders.

We have no existence until we reassemble the great path that crumpled to deliver us.

We are heart-stopping, as in our hearts can stop at any moment, and this is why we are so desperate to prove that we have existed at all.

If you trip near the edge of this problem, shed your weight, and it could be flight you have found.

WE ARE ARROWS #199

Dangle your regards from the bound and bolted wood, acknowledge that the mud beneath you is never hardening for your pleasure, and if the wind can give you a good enough shimmy to be pried loose from your only entry, you should know that you will simply lay there forever.

You were never part of the tree.

You will never be part of the mud.

We are unique in our community, but we must first make claim for each other.

WE ARE ARROWS #202

The fade is a disappearance, not a clearing of smoke, and if we choose to be physical at the bottom of the mouth of this world, it will do very little to change the telling of our story.

When we build houses it makes us appear strong. When we build doors it makes us appear inviting.

When we lock those doors our project of fear is complete.

We are too afraid to allow ourselves to become dust, adjustable in any waves of wind that may finds us.

We prefer to become fire, and then become smoke, but the clearing of our arrival leaves scorched earth.

We don't fade.

We spread like crop without harvest.

We are top-heavy.

We arch, bowing to our own imperfect grasp of what this world can do for us.

WE ARE ARROWS #203

Justifiable violence, we have shaken our heads in front of one pine tree and named it a forest.

We are comfortable with elegy, because we are comfortable with death.

Like nostrils adjusting to an alien scent, there was only so long we could be this destructive without permeation.

All hearts are separate with intent and it takes a great story to sew them back together…

Or that is what we tell ourselves when we have stripped the bark from the pine to wrap our vacant bodies with explanation.

WE ARE ARROWS #211

The silt spreads the shadows over the frozen retention ponds; the truth about what happens to the light dirt once the hole has been dug is an awful one.

We feel like silt sometimes.

We feel displaced without any real movement because, in fact, we have been placed somewhere foreign to us.

Some of us can make that home.

Some of us are unable to see anything but the borders that surround where we are from.

We are from the air over where we want most to be made whole.

We have no name for that place.

WE ARE ARROWS #214

We are exaltations, falling from the sun, and when we are quiet enough we can hear each plunge into the roar of each lion of this world.

We are almost never quiet enough to hear anything other than our own descent.

We are a celebration of competing sounds, and when our molecules collide wildly enough it can become music.

WE ARE ARROWS #219

That stage of emptiness we feel trailing us at all times, that is a powerful collection of imagined growth.

We are almost completely behind us, always mostly invisible to our own eyes.

We are pointed forward.

We are the anticipation of action and the sentiment to explain the dimple and the cut of our arrival.

We should, with our inherent violence, be more dedicated to regaining the paradise of the sky.

We should have no fear of getting lost in that storm.

We have always returned from our flights.

We have registered greatly amongst the stars.

༺ 🖐 ༻

ALL THE BIRDS ARE LEAVING

༺ 🖐 ༻

ALL THE BIRDS ARE LEAVING #1

First occasion of the dark squeeze,
the pressure that feels most of all
like a door closing, you panic—

all of your paths shake violently
at the simple thought that there will
be more winter than you have fire

& such accounting will have you
on the floor. If you stay there,
you will die there. The math won't

matter anymore. First occasion
of your fight, you want to love
everything forever, you want force

to become something too full to ever
bend. This is human ocean. This time
has no record, only moon and song.

ALL THE BIRDS ARE LEAVING #2

If it is, that this scene
is all shore, all give
& return to take back

more of what was once
only discard, then it is
the children, always willing

to partially bury our bodies,
that know best, that behave
according to the times.

They are securing
their elders. They are
dancing like we are gone

already. They see surf
as celebration. I do too,
but I am too tired to dig.

Darren C. Demaree

ALL THE BIRDS ARE LEAVING #3

Our blood crackles, always learning
so much more about fire than those things
that can never burn. We understand

that water is more important than gold,
but we never ever choose to piss accordingly.
We are still here, that does not mean

we cannot be forced out. There will be
three whistles. There will be one singer.
The many empty hands will applaud this.

ALL THE BIRDS ARE LEAVING #4

It works best
when we are
possessed by

a strange beauty,
a blank, un-decided
sky, a thought

of never leaving,
of second
& third words.

As long as we are
singing about it, we
are not mourning.

ALL THE BIRDS ARE LEAVING #5

Our clock,
the counting
has no place

for un-reality
& since the river
keeps no black,

keeps no white
either, we are
lucky indeed

that our best
moments
appear surreal,

accompanied
forever
by this haunt.

ALL THE BIRDS ARE LEAVING #6

We do not want to touch
the whole world, we want
the whole world to touch us

& if that is true then our good
relationship with time, slashed
through the sky that it is,

is purely decoration. Flush
to the flesh of our own light,
our race is one of waiting

in one place, our salvation
is roughed up, shoveled into
the artistry of accepting all.

ALL THE BIRDS ARE LEAVING #7

I have lost count of the beautiful lines
of this world,

their hook and dragging
of my own body has been pure,

ecstatic times. I am caught forever
by it. I will never be home

& I will always be at home
with the biting jewelry of the stars

dangled from my lip.
If I allowed this process to be forgotten,

then everything would fall apart.
If I rested, the only action would be

in the temporary grasses, where shade
is a feeding ground. I have been taken

by such artistry, by time continuing.

ALL THE BIRDS ARE LEAVING #8

Left, as in a piece
of the sun that started
as a smear of heat

& remains to ask
questions of the shadow,
because everything

wants to understand
the plusses & minuses
of their least comforting

position. I want to know
what happens when
warmth is never known

& then sneaks into the bath
of human experience
like a toe & then a body

whole, overwhelming.
It would be brutal
to be taken by such glory.

ALL THE BIRDS ARE LEAVING #9

You want death nine times
before you want to hear
that life will never end, that birds,

when they fly away they do so
only to return with a prize
in their mouths. You want me

to confirm your own ending
& to tell you what is in the bird's
mouth. It's berries that could kill

you, but the birds eat them like candy.
Take comfort in the first salvation
which is being born at all.

Take heart in the second salvation,
which is a full death, surrounded
by birds that will live forever.

Darren C. Demaree

ALL THE BIRDS ARE LEAVING #10

Without terror, can we only say
that we appreciate the uncountable
times the most? The fugue state

of happiness has us fixed upon
the river in the distance, and if we
never taste the traveling waters

we can always say we saw first
where the land bent to allow
the stream to escape from us.

Content with the dark times,
we never know what to do
with light, but we were born

knowing that one moment can be
enough landmark to name everything
after such an ecstatic filling of self.

ALL THE BIRDS ARE LEAVING #11

Driven by rage, our breathless style
of living accumulates losses like sticks
in a country fire, like something seen

from the road and never understood
by a member of the caravan. We are
& therefore, we are angry at this fact.

It takes good translation of the sky
to understand that any flight seen
is a flight returning to smoke.

Darren C. Demaree

ALL THE BIRDS ARE LEAVING #12

How rare it is to burrow
past the planted fields
& cozy home gardens,

all of them decorated
to please, then feed
& then please us again,

but to go deeper, past
the gold of our millennia
& call upon the shadows

of our steady feet,
would that be a blessing
as well? We want to rise

above our own dead,
because we don't want
to join them; that fear

is a great tangent.
Inexpressible, the good
barricades of our world

will vanish. We will meet
the numbers of our faith
& then have only ourselves

to define this whole dance.
Hill to valley to deep water,
we will still be right here.

ALL THE BIRDS ARE LEAVING #13

All forms of the morning,
the loss or beauty of new sun
masked as old sun, carrying

the baggage of the flame
like a champion racer
or the stuntman he will become

& each time we remember
to count the scars in the sky
the engine of the world

idles, it frightens us with quiet.
Accept that because we circle
a ball of fire, because the fire

gives us life, that anything
can happen, even in winter,
when we most desire safe footing

there can be whole sheets
of reality removed by one flare,
one bad lap of renewal.

ALL THE BIRDS ARE LEAVING #14

Our hope is the best
forgetting.

ALL THE BIRDS ARE LEAVING #15

Our least tender carbons
would swell into community
if the wind didn't rush us,

didn't layer our flash
& decay on the gravel drives
& lowered tree branches

of this world. When winter
comes and a snow flake lands
on my tongue, I know it is you,

your unique loss, your small gift
to time and to me. I'll take
anything that brings us closer.

ALL THE BIRDS ARE LEAVING #16

The blood is counted
& if we can ever do
the math on the ultimate

number, will we continue
to track the invalid losses
attributed to simple escape?

We know how many cups
of coffee we have each day.
The bottle counts martinis

for us. We find no joy
for those around us, simply
leaving without any fear.

We have no fingers to handle
that, and no numbers
to paint how incredible it is

to be free of the process.

Darren C. Demaree

ALL THE BIRDS ARE LEAVING #17

Most of all
are you alive
enough to take

your fear
of the fading
obligation,

to be everything
& leave behind
everything?

The best of us
leaves holes
that can be filled

by the right storm
the right water
or a good, bright

stone. I want
the river to dry
when I go,

but that is
the worst part
of my own fear.

ALL THE BIRDS ARE LEAVING #18

It could be wax
& only so much
splendor for each

of our deserved
shores. The water
counts our taste,

dips us in summer,
allows us to harden
before we, immersed

in reality, bend
to the hallucination
that we are sealed

to save forever. We
are temporary trophies,
never to be shelved.

Darren C. Demaree

ALL THE BIRDS ARE LEAVING #19

The rock and you,
time, if gently

filled, can be
as alive as your bones,

which are brimming
with life

& as sturdy a prop
as is available to us.

We only feel
our bones

when they are broken
& with time

it is the same thing,
with time we return

only after the great pain
of filling dark spaces

with swallowed light
that is almost certainly

stolen to be planted
& snapped into place.

We all limp, until we find
the processional.

ALL THE BIRDS ARE LEAVING #20

We are given more
than one word
& August arms

to split that word
into good definition
& a defiant religion

for any moment.
We have whole times
sparse with the length

& width of shoulders
that were chosen
for us. Strength

is mostly a myth,
but not enough of one
to remove

the importance
of strength. Be strong
in time's frame.

The picture
is entirely you,
your effort and dance.

ALL THE BIRDS ARE LEAVING #21

The numbers took the finger
& pointed it in our direction,
it filled the clouds with light,

meaning that rain is the point
of darkness. We are stunned
& we open our mouths. We are

thirsty and we open our mouths.
We are willing to be the variable
in the equation as long as we can

remain deaf to any countdown.
If we are taken away from fresh
falling, our smell will be obnoxious

& with that, the lovely surprises
of when and how the river finds us
will no longer be an outcome.

ALL THE BIRDS ARE LEAVING #22

We see the wings dance.
We hear the un-tempered
songs, fat with everything

& none of us are happy.
We are watching
the experience, waiting

to be filled by it. This regret
has no beautiful lining,
no celestial bargaining

& if we only learn the nevers
of flight, we will be buried
as dust without wind.

ALL THE BIRDS ARE LEAVING #23

We are recording the detriment
of our own fear,

always discussing hope abstractly,
always telling stories

about how we once held it gently
& didn't even realize

when it had gone. Hope
is as ornery, panicked

& as real as you are. It is abstract
only in that we cannot ever keep it

long enough to name it directly.
Hope burns. Hope can drown.

Hope is looking for a nest
that it can place inside of you

& if it uses everything you've got
to stay warm, then your heat

was never useless. I don't know
why you would ever think that.

ALL THE BIRDS ARE LEAVING #24

I have thoughts of un-reality,
bold digs for light children,
as in children bathed in light,

held in the mouth of the wind,
carried in long-lasting flights
that show them all of the queries

& struggles below their thin skins
& warm errors. I have thoughts
of un-reality, where time greets

our children with firm smiles
& immerses them in the good
hallucination of a proper distance

from our straining, our spills
of essence waiting for one sunset
to clear us of our wrongness

& acceptance of our wrongness.
We could be monsters. They will
greet us as monsters when given

back to the level of the field.
They could still love us.
They could hold us with all

of the parts of their small arms.
Children love monsters
when they're quiet and still.

ALL THE BIRDS ARE LEAVING #25

We don't want a finger,
we want whole hands,
to be puppeted by good,

but once you get the alien
feeling that what moves
inside of you dances

to a deep bass, the march
of time becomes all hips
& prostration bends to move

that feeling deeper inside,
to make it the face
on your guts, a smug lining

that feels uncontrolled.
There should be dancing
all the time. There should

be deep bass. The questions
about what moves us are slight
& irrelevant, if we're beautiful.

If it's going to be a mess,
let's put our arms in the air
& look each other in the eyes.

ALL THE BIRDS ARE LEAVING #26

If we can split the fact of time
into falling feathers, the spinning
of which would never blanket

our view of the sky, would our hearts
be calm with the stars, remove
the panic of the disappearing sun

& if we ever caught the discard
of a righteous flight in our teeth,
would our stories not last forever?

Darren C. Demaree

ALL THE BIRDS ARE LEAVING #27

Like watching a bird sing
& claiming the songs
don't contain any real words,

because it's not a song
that actually helps explain
why the bird is singing, it

becomes a story then that can't
happen to you. I have begun
to speak out loud to the dead,

asked my grandfather questions
without regard for his wither
& decay. I believe the questions

are real. I do not believe
the answers matter. I don't
think there are any answers,

but I know that when a bird sings,
there is always a horrible moment
when it looks like it might not.

ALL THE BIRDS ARE LEAVING #28

Once they reach past
the high branch
or the bus stop roof,

we want to be what fills
their hollow bones,
we want to be taken,

but be heavy enough
to never leave
our lonely bridges

that always hold fast
to what we love most,
our distance from each

other, our good sight
of the shape of each
other. We want to see

everything. We cannot
fly forever because of our
hammering want

to touch each other.

ALL THE BIRDS ARE LEAVING #29

Always reflective, the list I keep
carries with it the lovers and friends
I lost by leaving through the bottle.

Those names remain, always in order
& even carrying this freedom,
I cannot erase a single name. I want

most of all to be free of all thick glass,
but I want also to forget those people
with time. That will be easier

I think to lose them again, to never
know that I never lost them
in the first place. Almost all time

is punishing, but time relents
just before the three hawks lower
you in pieces, into the mud of the river.

ALL THE BIRDS ARE LEAVING #30

Endlessly, we are ending
introductions of the empty
motions. When we move

our arms we want the wind
to know our power. If we are
still here and unrecognized,

our shimmering will be effort
& effort again to leave
more than panicked kicks

that effected no butterflies
& changed no curl of winter.
We look crazy most of the time

& that is our greatest quality,
that we can demonstrate so
excitedly, our love of anything.

Darren C. Demaree

ALL THE BIRDS ARE LEAVING #31

Elbows tucked in, our roll through
the tops of these trees is short-lived,
but once we are in the river, we know

why we should have landed in the field.
If we were any fuller of grand attempts
to leave here and remain alive

our thin cloth would simply drape
the berry bushes, would cover fruit
that mattered. We were not sentenced,

we were gifted these trials by
the perfect number on the perfect day.
We are the most beautiful fraction

& every effort to delay or count
differently weighs the sky down, pushes
it harder against our thickened chests.

ALL THE BIRDS ARE LEAVING #32

Imagine one bird
held an instrument,
a violin, and could

play it beautifully,
but the weight of it,
the violin took flight

away from the bird,
how quickly would
the bird leave

the violin once winter
came upon the bird?
This is the one question

we could never answer.
Grasping a tree-limb,
our dedication to beauty

would prohibit us from
ever admitting that
we aren't making music,

that the wood
in our shaking hands,
is almost useless.

Darren C. Demaree

ALL THE BIRDS ARE LEAVING #33

There is always tea in the kettle
& even if the steam seems to chase

the birds, do we doubt the potency
of what remains on the heating?

I am here. I am licking the cups
so they will shine on this cloudy day.

ALL THE BIRDS ARE LEAVING #34

If we can assure the voice
that volume is flight,

why do the physics
of such weight hinder

the majesty of the robin?
The killing birds

never speak until the meal
is over. The songbirds

are always resting
on the lowest-hanging

branch. That is why
silence is always best?

That is why good singing
always feels like a feast.

ALL THE BIRDS ARE LEAVING #35

If today is the day
to walk towards
the sad, diverted

questions, the bold
ones that dictate
to us limitations

& absolute belief
in those limitations,
why should our lips

be closed to the other
sounds? Whistle.
Sing, damn you, open

your mouth widely
with a great noise.
If you receive

any answers
you will not be able
to swallow them

& so, why not sing?
Make up new words
& make your questions

a part of your day
that you can forget
or costume with hope.

Darren C. Demaree

ALL THE BIRDS ARE LEAVING #36

Where do the fountains go
when we have filled them
with our shiny wishes? Tossed

to believe, the kick of water
will be underwhelming
if the good mood should strike

the skirts and those of us
that chase any leg movement.
The cement will be rich

& we will be walking on money,
but no more will the adrenaline
give our youth a demonstration.

The water will drown in metal.
Whatever statue of whatever hero
will blink for the first time

& no more will we learn the joy
of walking somewhere dry,
soaked with the best of life.

ALL THE BIRDS ARE LEAVING #37

My hands are colder
because I have waved

them frantically
away from my heart?

No. I danced poorly
next to the cliff

where all flight
is decided upon

& without any gloves
their nakedness

brought only emotion
& no real action.

ALL THE BIRDS ARE LEAVING #38

If I wanted to know
how every famous painter
died, how they framed

their death, how much
violence it took to rip
those last moments away

from their gilded forearms
& horrible innards,
would that map for me

how best to die
when my own grip
weakens? I want to know

how to be alone
with death, because I know
already how to make

something that must happen
hate that is happening
as ugly as I can make it.

There can be grace, with time,
grace can take shoulders
& relax them, but not mine.

ALL THE BIRDS ARE LEAVING #39

If we move less,
we remember
more? This is

the same as being
born with a hand
around your throat

& never bothering
to free your voice.
Migrate, if only

to return home.
Dance, if only
to wake yourself.

Tell your stories
with one great lie
just to be ornery.

The hands you
were born with
will applaud.

Darren C. Demaree

ALL THE BIRDS ARE LEAVING #40

Because it will always be shapeless
& never give in to the wink
& swelling our own bodies do,

it is a good thing that we accommodate
the vagaries of our most scenic
of deities, time? Shall we build

& never finish a statue in honor of time?
Shall we embrace the heroism
of our ruling meter without ever once

using everything we've got to keep
everything we want? Forever? No?
I just want a better name for the beast.

ALL THE BIRDS ARE LEAVING #41

I have dwelled
& I have desired
to dwell more

in that desiring
focus. I have
found spirit

in an orange peel
& that confirmed
all of my loves.

ALL THE BIRDS ARE LEAVING #42

If we cannot touch the cuttlefish bone
with our tongues, if the bone is still inside
the fish & the fish is still alive, still

swimming away from our eager hands
& tongues, our gullets with such unsubtle
acids, then why are we still fishing here?

This is the same thing as asking why we
cannot swallow time. This is the same
thought we have while time swallows us.

This is why we move so quickly
when the water rises to meet our thighs,
because we are too afraid to be tasted

& left behind, un-whole in the river.
I was born un-whole. I would love to be
left here un-whole, my bones a prize.

Darren C. Demaree

ALL THE BIRDS ARE LEAVING #43

Like we have no protection
for the original flesh, our cork
was only the first rumor of aging

& as we have always been exposed
to the undulating elements
of every neighbor of this moment

& this moment, the footprints
of every moment have beaten a path
across our faces. We are still

beautiful, because we recognize
the second rumor of aging,
that it is something you do alone.

ALL THE BIRDS ARE LEAVING #44

Ninety-four calls
are the answer

to the same query,
forward, we go

forward with heart
that we are anti-scenic,

we are the scene
& it's our momentum

that makes us chose
what to love

enough to bring
with us. Ninety-four

actions with ninety-
four accompanying

emotions, not one
of which can be

buried without a schism
in the busiest of fields.

If you find a mound
of dirt without a marker,

run to the tree-line.
There is new story there

& one of the ninety-four
will lightning you home.

ALL THE BIRDS ARE LEAVING #45

Scuff the field,
the whole field,
do it with your toes

& then again
with your elbows
& then again

with your wild,
indelicate, reaching,
particle of a soul.

ALL THE BIRDS ARE LEAVING #46

As we know it,
what we want
most is not light,

it is the removal
of dark. The song
of it is boring.

I want ridiculous
beams of color
to warm the dark

& I want nothing
to question such
tremendous dance

& cover. There is
only darkness after,
but there is almost

every color in black,
only the cowards
don't believe that.

Darren C. Demaree

ALL THE BIRDS ARE LEAVING #47

I have taken off,
a headlong thrill,
I have no idea

what will happen
next & if I did,
I would not have

blown with wind,
I would have flicked
the bend-bound

fragments of my own
best understanding,
I would love

discovering
that I can fly
only with the sun

that is always finding
a way to be buried
at the extent

of the field's hold.
I have taken off
& that is the victory.

ALL THE BIRDS ARE LEAVING #48

We cannot touch
to throw
ourselves into

the permanence
of this shaggy,
whispering walk

& any projection
of ourselves
into the firmament

requires the sun
to bow to us
& that is the rare

opposite
of everything
I have learned.

Darren C. Demaree

ALL THE BIRDS ARE LEAVING #49

The lines on my face
are so much more
about the wind-streaked

blessings I have collected
than the constant dawn
of time overwhelming

the loose pockets
of my skin, though both
have allowed me

to collect a tremendous
darkness, which bobs
to weave through

the glory of my best signal.
I am one being, held warm
by another's shine.

My pleasant appearance
looks best clouded by
a horribly crowded beard.

ALL THE BIRDS ARE LEAVING #50

What is this field
without fidelity
to rock or crop

or titan cloak
of black fullness?
It is a field.

It owes you nothing.
It yields, giving
without a particle

of solid reasoning.
We are the same
as this thick space.

ALL THE BIRDS ARE LEAVING #51

Screaming for the echo,
I have placed hours against
my hips to memorize

the count of good lingering
& to learn the poverty
of my own motion. On

my back, I want most of all
to share everything I have
& to be left here, giving.

Darren C. Demaree

ALL THE BIRDS ARE LEAVING #52

We are without
promise
& going elsewhere

would be awful
acceptance
of a deal spoken
in numbers
by clouds

that hold nothing,
no color to warm
our blue violence
towards belief.

I hold time
lightly,
I have plans
to make us

whole
with empathy
for the field.

We are crop,
yes, yes, yes,
we are risen
to sustain
the equation
of a great beat,

a heart's
determination

to remove
the brutal frame
of our one query.

ALL THE BIRDS ARE LEAVING #53

I know what's wrong
with our fingering,

the counting is never
sexual enough to coax

a response from the clouds
& if you are merely tapping

moments from your skin
into nothing, no flesh,

than why elevate the poke
to prod the vanishing air?

If you must bow,
make it part of a motion

that ends in the lifting
of someone else's tender

buttons. Time has
nothing tender; it takes

other people to create
worth in such a passing.

ALL THE BIRDS ARE LEAVING #54

If we could hear the numbers
through the keyhole of the universe,
the firm, magical digits that dance,

that give us dances, would we spend
less time gesticulating towards the sky
with anger? I think it's good for us,

to hear only a whisper of the divine
equations. We are better at grasping
than we will ever be at holding starlight.

ALL THE BIRDS ARE LEAVING #55

I had one thought
about cupping
my hands, duct-taping

them together, removing
my fingerprints first
with long-stick matches

& then shielding the ground
with my own tarp(ed) hands
& then allowing nothing

to grow beneath
my identity-free shield
& then I thought

about what would grow
in my hands. Nothing.
I had one thought

about cupping my hands
for a drink of water
from the sky. It was good,

I think, to yield
the control of the elements
& allow thick nature.

I am thankful
to live so far
from the hardware store.

Darren C. Demaree

ALL THE BIRDS ARE LEAVING #56

Soon is the dot
that feels ruin
first, the fields

take your best seed
& then what?
Soon? Never

does our day
mature past intent
& even that is only

an idea of a feeling
before the blood comes.
We see soon,

we are surrounded
by the almost reality
of soon, but rarely

does it give any crop
worth putting in
our mouths, our first

soul weakens
with anticipation
& rarely steels itself

for all weather
& all waiting,
the unending promise

that is kept
unending by place,
never by our nature.

ALL THE BIRDS ARE LEAVING #57

There is no firmness
in the equation world,

but there is always action
to be had, clumsy action,

wringing to count time
action to desert the action,

no matter. Could it be
any more than what we

asked for? No, but to ask
is to act, to put only one

hand into our pie. Join me,
please, with the other

hand, your face, now
your face. Let's enjoy

this metaphor fully,
let's consume the world

& understand that when
our mouths meet, it's to share.

Darren C. Demaree

ALL THE BIRDS ARE LEAVING #58

Designed to be holes
filled with the wrong
numbers, sky numbers

for a dirt world, our
layering of perspectives
has become weighted

with every swing
of gravity's patchwork.
We are sewn beauty,

that does not mean
we cannot meet the oil
& the orphan of our star's

best intentions, that we
exist, that our hearts
are soft enough

for real magic
to become planted
in each of our bones.

ALL THE BIRDS ARE LEAVING #59

On, on, on, our knuckles
count mountains,

thin white into gold
& wild the canary

into a beast that owns
the mineshaft.

We never needed
monsters, but we gave
the casual

a monster's name
so when we made
it to a Tuesday,

we could be
called heroes.
There is enough

world in my hands
already. The scars
there are from times

when I did not
believe such things,
when my grip

leaked on, on, on
my knuckles, their count
limitless with ecstatic

fictions of my greatness.

Darren C. Demaree

ALL THE BIRDS ARE LEAVING #60

It's one growth
from the grove
of the ear, an echo

that gives eyes
to time, teaches it
that though the tree

becomes the sky,
surrendering
to the canvas

unlimited, the tree
still holds the song
of our first attention.

We strain, always,
for a message
from the stars

& though the birds
appear headed
that direction,

we should consider
first, where they
make their home,

where their voice
first reached past
the root system.

Flush to the oak,
if you hear anything
it is the truth.

ALL THE BIRDS ARE LEAVING #61

I take part in the violence
that scatters answers
by living for four things

instead of three, by loving
myself as much as I love
you.   I want to love more

than that, but I would never
allow my arms to move past
my own body. I am selfish

sometimes, but that is never
damning. I want to fly
& love everything from above,

where my love means more
to me. I want to exist
without wanting anything,

but I have passed the point
of paraphrase, I have been
given a full sentence

& I must decide how to be
absolute. I must find actual
strength, in your arms

& find the perfect words
to thank you for never doubting
where I would land.

Darren C. Demaree

ALL THE BIRDS ARE LEAVING #62

The beauty arrived,
that does not mean
the beauty is gone,

or has fallen off, loosed
into the elements
& just because the birds

are leaving, that does
not mean the beauty is,
that means that we

should maybe think
about leaving the beauty
behind us, because us,

our eyes, can find
any treasure to claim
as a good weight.

Let us follow the birds.
They rarely drown
in the glow of their own

collections. They keep
what they need
in their tight chests.

ALL THE BIRDS ARE LEAVING #63

Thing
that we cannot touch,

you are strangely warm
to us,

but if there is no room
between your progression

& our own,
could you relent

your call-less march,
so that we can collect

this mess?
We love your prod,

un-gentle as it is,
but we have

lost so many
swellings in your wind

& we cannot remember
why

we were so ecstatic,
or what we did

next
that abandoned

the scene
so completely.

Darren C. Demaree

ALL THE BIRDS ARE LEAVING #64

There are animals
that keep treasure

in their bellies
& though some of us,

our old leaders,
looked as if they did,

too, we are judged
rarely for what we can

swallow. Thin-
throated, our counting

of time isn't keeping
time, it's naming it

before we even know
what it is. I remember

etc., is our best
closeness to thick

reality. The sinew
we will never see,

but we have infinite
names for that, too.

ALL THE BIRDS ARE LEAVING #65

We are the seed
& the crop.

We are subject
to each season

& if there are
a thousand suns

& a billion stars,
we will still only

rise one time
& be consumed

during the flight
of one bird,

too excellent
to be frozen

by this process.

Darren C. Demaree

ALL THE BIRDS ARE LEAVING #66

This is not the finishing
of one long fuse
connected to one large

explosion of self
lumped against, lumped
on time. This is

seven billion fuses
of various lengths,
all of them imitating

the sound of sizzle
we hear when we are
alone. Make the sound.

Do you see any birds
while you make it?
That could mean

anything, really, it could,
but for a second,
how much pleasure

did you hold,
by knowing you are lit
& contact is waiting?

ALL THE BIRDS ARE LEAVING #67

Coiled red, we are always trying
to escape our last escape attempt
from the embarrassment we feel

for feeling so selfish when asked
about the possible storm of our own
end. When we are headed back

to the carbon, our response
is personal, but why? Release!
Say, after what was everything

that you knew, I wish for you
to feel no clock other than the first
& I hope you never care more

about your own collapsing eyes
than you do about the spectacular
forces that gave you a narrative.

ALL THE BIRDS ARE LEAVING #68

Curse of the window,
I am a part of the world
& I am incredible

& thick with loneliness,
as I see so many epics
developing without me

& that is the sort of fear
that removes joints
from men. I was afraid

of being broken
& then, I was afraid
of never being whole.

Now, when I see a leak
of beasts, escaping into
the sky, I flap my arms

& believe whatever
I can believe when I am,
when my body moves

so rapidly that intent
becomes the last part
of my given nature.

ALL THE BIRDS ARE LEAVING #69

Shrug the oil,
intimate as it
can be, before

the ecstatic dip
of time waterfalls
away your best

dirt. You will
dig the mess
during this art-

ful loss of body,
but you will love
that moment

when someone,
even yourself,
believes wholly

that your ripple
is actual beauty
being delivered.

Darren C. Demaree

ALL THE BIRDS ARE LEAVING #70

Or fullness
beating you,

all the time
it's good

to be a little
bit hungry

& in beating
searches

for fullness
that fills

only enough
to costume

your ultimate
knowledge,

that an ache
is not a pain

& the strength
of a tsunami

builds
from still water

stirred by beaks
of endurance.

ALL THE BIRDS ARE LEAVING #71

Left alone, we are
shrines, partly
observed by the float

& eye of numbers
that are never the same
as they were

the night before
you found belief
in the celestial formula

& the direct correlation
of how quickly animals
leave your side

when the day begins.
Nothing is ruined,
nothing ever will be

& our best, warm
nothing, will never
be the same again,

you know that, right?

ALL THE BIRDS ARE LEAVING #72

(Take this quilt,
this stored warmth

& admire only
who held it last?)

I am on the coast
of all of humanity

& I am still strong
in this robbing wind,

because the rest
of you were strong

before I knew it
was coming for me.

ALL THE BIRDS ARE LEAVING #73

Without any tangle

above the sub-atomic level,
we are only

collisions to each other

& a short tenderness,
enough to allow hope

before we separate

into two leavings
& no staying.

I understand this

& it means nothing
to me. Come here, please.

Darren C. Demaree

ALL THE BIRDS ARE LEAVING #74

Blinking to the sparrow's song
will not give you the rhythm
to do more than miss half

of everything, but then again,
to be constantly serenaded
& surprised all the time,

could be held correctly as gift
or as panic. Could you,
just once, pay attention

to nature without wanting
to be part of it? Every surface
sleeps with the images

& notes of simple beauty,
a song un-interrupted by words
that will always feel like salvation

because this singer
will not be able to color
the damning with a narrative.

ALL THE BIRDS ARE LEAVING #75

Joiners, driven
& understood
not through any

night in church,
but as round
muscles thinning

in the sky
as demonstration
of an absurd faith

that we will
never be alone
if we present

ourselves
to the world
as a risk

to ourselves.
Leap! We rally
best to the fallen.

Darren C. Demaree

ALL THE BIRDS ARE LEAVING #76

I have no memory
of you

sucking down air
while everyone

else
promised

to wrap their cotton
arms around

the silent birds,
to chuck the birds

that could not sing
fast enough

that the wind's
reaction

would sing
for them. I have

no memory
of you being

there. You must
be one of them,

one
of the good people.

ALL THE BIRDS ARE LEAVING #77

Express alive, ruin
the sky with you,

your dance, love
the time to know

that knowing stops
a good rhythm.

ALL THE BIRDS ARE LEAVING #78

Because we are recording
this song

& dance, we will never be
lost more than when we

cannot buy the recordings.
I have heard a voice,

glowing with praise,
but I was never able

to own the voice
that could repeat

the phrases. I dance more
now, just in case

the warming gives spirit
to time. It doesn't,

but my hustle must please
somebody,

because no mountains
have moved to stop me.

It is never the same song,
or the same dance,

but I have faith
that my sweat

will grow to hold
any boat, any tide.

ALL THE BIRDS ARE LEAVING #79

I am learning
more

not to compare
anything

to fruit,
especially time

which arrived
before us,

ripe
& arrived

ready to leave
the vine,

almost an oil
already,

we were born
mid-flight

in a bath
of spoil,

- 195 -

but that's why
I am learning

to love
everything,

even as it turns
into the smell

of having been.

ALL THE BIRDS ARE LEAVING #80

How tremendous
the fury

of the dial
that was turned

many times
before

& that now,
we are counting

as an animal
we can return

to spring
& keep there

forever.
Ding. Let's

begin again.
This time

was my time
& there is no

cold wine
that can extend

my meal
into the next.

Darren C. Demaree

ALL THE BIRDS ARE LEAVING #81

Skimming
for depth,
I ate small

parts of time,
tucked them
in my belly

& gave life
to nothing,
but belief

that appetite,
the behavior
of it,

dictates
less than
a mask worn

around
no holiday.
It's something

to give into
when hands
are seasonal

demons
that shovel
light effort.

ALL THE BIRDS ARE LEAVING #82

We invented leather
so that we could have
a leather strap un-buckling,

so that we could record
how long it takes to strap
back up the leather,

so we knew how little
to care about how slowly
we un-did leather straps.

We have committed such
glorious traps for our minds
& bodies, they confirm

everything good
& curious about us
& our general leanings.

ALL THE BIRDS ARE LEAVING #83

Hard laugh, uncomfortably
comfortable
with our connection

to nothing, we must allow
our draining spirits
to firework

before we line the rivers
with our discontent
& our failed bodies.

If you are counting the times
where your number ecstatic
raised your blood

to a level of memorable
consequence,
then you have

already given up.
Spark of our lives, violently
unknowing of reason,

I feel divided
only because when I stand
barefoot in the mud,

nothing grows around me.
This is why I stare
so resolutely at the lightning

as it dances, rooted
in nothing
but the spectacular.

ALL THE BIRDS ARE LEAVING #84

The eyes
behind
the glasses

trust
the glasses
more

than
the hands
trust

the muscles
trust
the sweat

that always
hovers
above

the great
effort
of intent.

ALL THE BIRDS ARE LEAVING #85

Framed
& cliff
bound,
I have

no desire
to challenge
the sun,
but to make

a single wave
my belief
in descent
must hold

true. If
I rise,
this
will become

a hallelujah
of disbelief
& I imagine
the clouds

will hold me
for too long.
We get to
choose

our burning,
to have that
taken,
an epic

cruelty.
Please,
don't leave
me

in the ocean.

ALL THE BIRDS ARE LEAVING #86

What does the cello
have to do
with the pause

before the wing
breaks into wind?
I don't know this.

I know how light
that beauty is,
though

& I read once
about a farmer
that played the cello

in his field
during droughts,
he said it was crop

when there
would be no
other crop.

We are all, always,
about to be song,
but that pause,

the tension of the notes,
resistant
to give us lift,

they are real crop
in any state
of nature.

ALL THE BIRDS ARE LEAVING #87

A relationship
with very little
penetration, we

are mostly action
for consequences
that take place

outside the sharp
numbers. We
arrived, so we

can say we came,
but our best hump
was saved

for the camel's
display.
This place is exact

& perfect in dirt
& a light touch,
fucking hysterical.

ALL THE BIRDS ARE LEAVING #88

Rest, honeycomb,
you are already filled
with recklessness

held tightly against
your sweet barriers.
If you are ever air-

born, it will be
your trail the birds
find. We will know

this by following
their simple songs.
They will leave us

the shell, again,
they will leave us
the work

of a framer.
It will be scene
of incredible hope.

Darren C. Demaree

ALL THE BIRDS ARE LEAVING #89

Falling questions,
my hands are tied
to the few stars

that smell as home
& if in your descent
your aim becomes full

with me, my chest
will be at the ready
to intertwine

with your maddening
ways. I have made
myself broad

through such small
actions. I have
answered nothing

that rises past
my own desperation.
I am still, like crop

young enough
to matter in the field,
worth nothing in any

real market, but this
feels, most often
like actual strength.

ALL THE BIRDS ARE LEAVING #90

Still fastened to the sun,
our cold snaps off

in the cantering mirror
that cares little

if we ever wear the mask
of the unconcerned.

Our reflection
is important, absolutely

never, but if it becomes
a source of light,

you should aim your nose
towards the ocean bottom.

Darren C. Demaree

ALL THE BIRDS ARE LEAVING #91

The impulse is to dissipate,
to interject oneself slowly
into the wind, as if being

carried away to be hung,
displayed like the cold moon,
as victory through image,

to loom over the field
& feel as if you are more so
than a perched figure

waiting to be acknowledged
fifty yards behind the action.
I have lost whole chunks

of myself. I have lost pieces
the wind could never lift.
I have done so taking risks

so great that their failing
has taken my own name
& I have never been

so complete. I move slowly
now, but I cover expanses
the same as any momentum.

ALL THE BIRDS ARE LEAVING #92

Complete root, pool
& dragging of the pool
to the extension

of our time together,
you are what was first
imagined to be angel

because you were joy
delivered without
expectation of joy;

the crowd that gathered
around us then were birds
dedicated to our saving.

ALL THE BIRDS ARE LEAVING #93

So many times
we have re-sold
ourselves on effort
& the jittering
strength
of unification,

that twenty billion
hands pressing
different points
of the world
is harmful. If we
all could choose

only one, wouldn't
the air release
quickly, like we
were all characters
on a children's
balloon? There is

panic in all of us
& we are counting
any sign
that swallows
renewal to be our
own demise as well.

Danger frightens
the animals away,
but so does music,
great music, played
loudly, indifferent
of the audience

& that is renewal
as well, the clearing
& the celebration,
the dancing
& the slow return
of our own animal.

ALL THE BIRDS ARE LEAVING #94

It's a mirror, the geography
I've drunk through electric
swoops of the good wings

of time. I have never stopped
counting, but I have stopped
caring about the numbers

splayed, rotating across my
width. My reach will fail
the pursuit. My muscles

will embrace the failing.
I will fly through every plain
& never rise above a mountain

that could be magic, if only
we allowed it to be. It's held,
this time, by all of us

& I never felt more
than I felt when you dropped
me from the first cliff,

believing as you did, that I
was supposed to follow
the birds. I never could,

but that was the lesson
we needed most, that we
get to stay here, together

for all of the un-definable.

Acknowledgements

The Aguilar Expression—We Are Arrows #82, We Are Arrows #83, We Are Arrows #84

Albatross—A Violent Sound in Almost Every Place #123

Bacon Review—All the Birds Are Leaving #74, All the Birds Are Leaving #75

Barefoot Review—A Violent Sound in Almost Every Place #129, A Violent Sound in Almost Every Place #130, A Violent Sound in Almost Every Place #132

Bare Root Review—A Violent Sound in Almost Every Place #147

The Binnacle—A Violent Sound in Almost Every Place #158

Brick Rhetoric—All the Birds Are Leaving #67, All the Birds Are Leaving #68, All the Birds Are Leaving #69

Confrontation—A Violent Sound In Almost Every Place #161

Cricket Online Review—A Violent Sound in Almost Every Place #62, A Violent Sound in Almost Every Place #63

Episodic—All the Birds Are Leaving #4, All the Birds Are Leaving #6

Homestead Review—We Are Arrows #94, We Are Arrows #95

Iodine—We Are Arrows #139, We Are Arrows #140

Ishaan Literary Review—A Violent Sound in Almost Every Place #56, A Violent Sound in Almost Every Place #57

IthacaLit—A Violent Sound in Almost Every Place #17, A Violent Sound in Almost Every Place #18

Lullwater Review—We Are Arrows #160

Mind(less) Muses —We Are Arrows #195

NoD—We Are Arrows #185

POEM—A Violent Sound in Almost Every Place #16

Pointed Circle—A Violent Sound in Almost Every Place

Posit—All the Birds Are Leaving #79, All the Birds Are Leaving #80, All the Birds Are Leaving #81

Pudding Magazine—A Violent Sound in Almost Every Place #207, A Violent Sound in Almost Every Place #208

Roanoke Review—All the Birds Are Leaving #54

Ship of Fools—A Violent Sound in Almost Every Place #59

Smoking Glue Gun—We Are Arrows #2

Spoon River Poetry—All the Birds Are Leaving #60

Stirring—We Are Arrows #25

Tiger's Eye—A Violent Sound in Almost Every Place #94, A Violent Sound in Almost Every Place #95

Umbrella Factory—We Are Arrows #7, We Are Arrows #8, We Are Arrows #9

Utter—All the Birds Are Leaving #7, All the Birds Are Leaving #8, All the Birds Are Leaving #9

Weber: The Contemporary West—All the Birds Are Leaving #64

Wilderness House—We Are Arrows #58, We Are Arrows #59, We Are Arrows #60

Writer's Bloc—We Are Arrows #109

Zymbol—We Are Arrows #71, We Are Arrows #72

About the Author

DARREN C. DEMAREE is from Mount Vernon, Ohio. He is a graduate of The College of Wooster and Miami University. He is the recipient of six Pushcart Prize nominations. Outside of his own poetry, Darren is the founding editor of *AltOhio* and *Ovenbird Poetry*, as well the managing editor of the *Best of the Net Anthology*. Currently, he is living and writing in Columbus, Ohio, with his wife and children. He is the author of several books and collections including, *As We Refer to our Bodies* (8th House Publishing, 2013), *Not for Art nor Prayer* (8th House Publishing, 2015). *Many Full Hands Applauding Inelegantly* is his sixth collection of poetry.